HOW TO CREATE MULTIPLE STREAMS OF INCOME

Buying Homes in Nice Areas With Nothing Down

Peter Conti & David Finkel

"This publication is designed to provide accurate and authoritative information in regard to the subject matter covered. It is sold with the understanding that the publisher is not engaged in rendering legal, accounting, or other professional service. If legal advice or other expert assistance is required, the services of a competent professional person should be sought."

From a Declaration of Principles jointly adopted by a Committee of the American Bar Association and a Committee of Publishers.

Cover and book design by Robert Aulicino

ISBN: 1-893384-15-2
Library of Congress Card Number
00-191529

Printed in the united states of america

10   9   8   7   6   5   4   3   2

DEDICATION

To my incredible family, for putting up with all the travel and late night coaching calls to students, and for supporting me as I live the life of my dreams. To David, who is my best friend and business partner, thank you for believing in me more than I thought possible. And to Dad, thanks for everything, especially when I feel loved by you.
—PETER CONTI

Thank you Peter for being my best friend and business partner. You are my mentor and have been such an uplifting role model in my life, both in terms of my business success and in my growth as an individual. I also want to give thanks to my family for supporting me, not just now with my business, but earlier too with my dreams of the Olympics. Thank you Heather for your love and support. Finally, I just wanted to tell the world how grateful I am for the many wonders that have come into my life these past few years. It's been an exciting time.
—DAVID FINKEL

Acknowledgments

Together, we would also like to say thank you to the following people who have been instrumental in the completion of this book:

Darcy Birkeland, Theresa Buck and Renata Burgess, who are not only incredible people but also very talented.

Paul Bauer, whose help editing the content of this book was extremely valuable and will help so many readers be more successful.

Barbara Giles, who helped uncover all those pesky little mistakes of spelling and grammar.

To the Real Estate Investor Associations, who help the average investor become so much more.

To our students, whose trust and faith in the system has been humbling. We admire your determination and are thrilled with your success. Thank you for being the literal laboratory to fine-tune all of these ideas.

To all of you, we want to again say thank you for the hours you've toiled so this book could touch the lives of hundreds of thousands of people.

CONTENTS

"What Would You
Attempt If You *Knew* You
Could Not Fail?"

FOREWORD

A New Way of Investing in Real Estate

Welcome to a new way of investing in real estate. This book will teach you how to create multiple streams of income buying homes in nice areas with nothing down. You won't need thousands of dollars and perfect credit to do it either. You can start where you are and with what you have and in 90 days or less you can be on the road to wealth.

When you are finished reading this book, you will be a different person in two specific ways. First, you are going to be what we call a "true believer." Being a true believer means you don't just understand that creating incredible wealth through real estate is possible, but you KNOW it is possible for YOU!

When I begin working with my real estate students, I am working for the day when they get that first check in their hand with the profits from their first deal. As they stare down at the large amount, I see a strange look come into their eyes. They look up and I can see that their life will never be the same. They know that they can create as much wealth as they want. They have the specific tools to do it. Money will never be a concern of theirs again. They understand that this stuff works. They are now what I call a true believer.

—PETER CONTI

Right now as you start this book you probably know that real estate is a great way to make money. You've talked with people who have done it. You've seen people in the media who have gone from rags to riches. You've probably even read a book or two about how people did it. But this isn't being a true believer. As a true believer, you know for yourself that you can use real estate to earn your fortune.

By the time you have finished this book, you are going to be a true believer. You will know in your gut that you can go out and within a few years, turn your financial dreams into your financial reality.

Second, you will know exactly what you need to do to put your new knowledge into action. You will have a proven success track to guide you. When you follow this track, your financial life will never be the same. You'll know you can create as much wealth as you choose. The only limits you will have are those you impose upon yourself.

We don't mean to sugar coat any of this—it takes work. If you're looking for the newest "get rich quick" craze, then you're looking in the wrong place. This book will teach you the timeless secrets of how to use real estate as your vehicle to financial freedom. It is going to take work, patience, and persistence. Are you prepared to put in an hour or two a day building your future? Are your dreams worth it? Is your family?

We will give you the same guarantee that we give to our workshop students: If you put these techniques and strategies to work for 1-2 hours a day for just 90 days, we guarantee you'll have your first (or next) investment property at a substantial profit. If not, simply write our office at 7475 W. 5th Ave., Suite 100, Lakewood, CO 80226, sharing your experience with us. Include a copy of your receipt from your purchase of this book, and we'll personally refund every penny you invested in buying this book. That's how strongly we believe in this system. It works. The only question is, will you?

INTRODUCTION

The Challenge

We knew that our methods worked. They had worked for our students and us across the country time and time again. We would, however, on occasion run across people who insisted that our ideas were just too good to be true. After all, they would say, how could you really buy nice homes with nothing down and such little risk?

It was frustrating. We would go out and speak to groups of investors who were convinced that while you could buy property with nothing down in the 1980s, you just could not do it in the late 1990s.

You see, the people who are used to investing the "traditional" way have a hard time seeing a totally different way to invest. It is different because it eliminates the pitfalls of traditional real estate, like negative cash-flow, maintenance headaches, and late rent checks, but still has the huge profit potential real estate has always offered. These investors were just working so hard at what they already knew that they were unable to take a step back and gain a new perspective. Sometimes working harder just isn't the answer—working smarter is.

We searched for a way to quiet these critics and help those people too scared to get going with real estate. We knew that if we could go into a city cold, with a select group of students and pick up a ton of properties, then we could show the skeptics and scared bystanders that you can still make thousands of dollars buying homes with nothing down.

13

"I kept wondering what could I do... what could I do... I pondered this question for months. One day while I was out for a hike in the wilderness behind my house, the answer came to me — issue a challenge and make good on it in front of the world. And then these words of the challenge flashed into my mind...

"Send me to any city with a select group of my students, and in three days each of my students will own or control a minimum of $250,000 worth of real estate using none of their own money."

As quickly as these words came into my mind, all the doubts came too. How could I possibly do this? What happens if I fail? Then I stopped myself, took a deep breath and looked out over the magnificent landscape in front of me. I was just coming over the top of a ridge and could see the valley spread out below me. I was startled when a pair of hawks soared over me and circled high in the sky.

I believe there are no accidents in life. This was a message from above that I needed to go after my dreams. One way or another, I would soar... I committed to the challenge."

—Peter Conti

We set off with our Challenge team to San Diego, California on December 8. We had chosen three beginning investors just a month earlier and had spent three days training them to use the Purchase Option system. Who were these three students of ours?

First there was Jim, a postman from Colorado. Jim was thankful for the steady work of the post office but dreamed of building more. His body was tired of the long days of lugging a 65-pound mailbag through the cold Colorado winter. He desperately wanted a way out, a way to create financial freedom.

Next there was Margaret, a single mother with three lovely daughters. Margaret worked as a maintenance technician for a local manufacturer. She had actually just signed her first real estate deal two days before joining us on the Challenge. Her powerful drive had pushed her to take the information she learned during our three-day intensive training and go out and put it to use.

Finally there was John, a retired minister. For years he had looked after the spiritual well being of thousands of people and now he wanted to build the financial base to take care of his wife and three children. John knew real estate was the way to go. He had even bought a course on "nothing down" investing advertised on television months before we ever met him. He just needed someone to take him by the hand and to show him exactly how to do it.

All three of our students arrived in San Diego excited, nervous, and ready to put some money-making deals together immediately. They weren't the only ones who were more than excited.

> "I have to be honest—I was scared when we got started. I knew my techniques worked. After all, I had used them to become a millionaire by age 35. But still this was an intimidating challenge to make good on."
>
> —Peter Conti

When all was said and done, we didn't just meet the Challenge goal of $250,000 of real estate for each of our students—we more than doubled it! That's right, over the three days we locked up over $1.5 million worth of real estate. And what did it cost us up-front to do it? Just $37 down!

Here's what Jim, Margaret, and John had to say about it:

"The biggest thing I got out of the experience was the confidence that I could go out there and do this myself. It's an amazing feeling to know that now I'm capable of making this kind of money with real estate."

—JIM E.

"It was amazing for me see the whole process from start to finish. I now know that I can go out there by myself and put these deals together."

—MARGARET U.

"Before I went on the Challenge, I had a gut-level doubt that this just wouldn't work. I mean it all sounded great in theory but I had hidden fears that nobody would actually sell you their house without up-front money. Now I know this stuff works. I know this because I've done it myself— not just once but ten times!"

—JOHN S.

Do you want to learn how to put the secret strategies and techniques we used on the Challenge to work building your bank account? Then you need to pour over every word of this book because for the first time ever, we are going to reveal the Purchase Option system to you.

But be forewarned! If you are not success oriented, if you don't have a prejudice towards action, then you might find this book very uncomfortable.

On the other hand, if creating wealth is your idea of fun, and helping people motivates you—we're going to have a great time together in this book! This is your chance to learn the inside secrets of how you can create multiple streams of income buying homes in nice areas with nothing down.

Overview

An Armchair Tour of Exactly What You'll Learn From This Book (And Why It Will Empower You to Change Your Financial Future Forever!)

In this book, you'll learn how the entire Purchase Option system works. There are three steps to any Purchase Option deal. Step one is for you to find a motivated seller of a property. This step is critical. By working with a motivated seller rather than with an ordinary seller, you will be able to create more profits and feel good knowing that you helped a seller in trouble solve his or her problems.

Step two is for you to meet with this motivated seller and figure out a win-win solution to their problems. The keys to this step are for you to accurately diagnose just what the seller's real needs are and to have enough options so that you can structure a profitable deal that meets those needs.

Step three is to sell the property to a new buyer. You are going to learn why tenant-buyers (people who are "renting to own") are the best people to put in the property. Why? Because a tenant-buyer gives you all the benefits of owning a rental property, such as, monthly cash flow and long-term appreciation. At the same time, it limits the downside, like maintenance hassles and late rent checks.

Section One:
How to Buy Homes in Nice Areas
with Nothing Down

Using the Purchase Option system, you'll learn how to create multiple streams of income buying homes in nice areas with nothing down. Once you sign up a property and find a tenant-buyer, you are just about done. You still have to cash the monthly checks you're earning, but other than that, you won't have much involvement at all. Your goal is to set up several of these properties so that you have multiple streams of residual income flowing to you on a continual basis. That's real wealth.

Wouldn't it be nice if your job was like this? Would you like to do the work once but get paid for it over and over? With Purchase Option investing you will! Because you took the time to learn how to set up the deal right, you get the reward of profits flowing to you long after you have stopped putting any more effort into the deal.

In this section you'll learn:
- The three simple steps in all Purchase Option deals
- How to enjoy all the benefits of owning property with none of the risks or hassles
- How you can make thousands of dollars helping motivated sellers solve their problems
- How to turn any home into a "rent-to-own" home and use it to create windfall profits for yourself
- Exactly how Purchase Option is *different* and *better* than all the old, outdated ways of investing in real estate

19

Section Two:
How to Find Motivated Sellers

The critical key to unlocking hundreds of thousands of dollars from real estate is finding a "motivated seller." A motivated seller is defined as a property owner whose major purpose in life at that precise moment is to find a way to get rid of his property.

When you find this motivated seller, not only will you make a lot of money, but more importantly you will feel good about being able to help solve his problems. That's one of the best parts of Purchase Option investing: helping people out.

Do you like to help people? Are you OK with getting paid to help people? You are? Great! Because that is the essence of Purchase Option investing—getting paid for crafting creative solutions to motivated sellers' real estate troubles.

In this section you'll learn:
- The seven reasons why motivated sellers sell
- What motivated sellers *really* want
- How to avoid the biggest mistake that the average investor makes
- How to turn your telephone into a money-making machine, which will save you time and help you avoid hours of frustration
- How to develop a "money farm" to make your investing more fun and more profitable
- How to set up money making relationships with realtors (with five techniques to turn these relationships into new paydays for you!)
- Money-saving AND money-making guerrilla marketing tactics to launch your investing business—*now!*

Section Three:
How to Get Motivated Sellers to Say "YES!" to Your Creative Offer

Once you have found your motivated seller, it's time to sit down with them to figure out how you can help them in a way that leaves them feeling good about the deal and makes you a healthy profit.

It takes a soft touch to draw out exactly what the seller's real needs are in a way that helps open their mind to your creative solutions. Remember, motivated sellers are often in a stressed emotional condition and you have to be very respectful and gentle in dealing with them.

There are specific questions you can ask to help "diagnose" the seller's real needs. You're going to learn these questions and how to use the answers to help the seller *and* you make money—lots of money.

In this section you'll learn:
* How to close a deal every time
* How to meet the seller's needs and maximize your prof its as well
* A little-known question that will get the seller to drop his price—instantly
* A secret 5-step system to get the seller to say "YES!" to your offer
* How to get an immediate answer from ANY seller
* Two secret words to get the seller to agree with your offer BEFORE you actually make it
* How to talk about money with the seller without blowing your deal
* A simple 4-step formula to get sellers to like you

21

Section Four:
How to Find Your Hungry Tenant-Buyer

Congratulations on getting a property locked-up! Now it's time for you to finish the final part of any Purchase Option deal: finding a tenant-buyer. Just what is a tenant-buyer? Well, you know what a tenant is—someone who leases or rents a property. And you know what a buyer is— someone who purchases the property. A tenant-buyer is someone who is "renting to own" a property.

The reason you are going to master the art of finding tenant-buyers is that it gives you all the benefits of having tenants, such as monthly cash-flow and flexibility, without any of the downside hassles. Unlike an average tenant, tenant-buyers will take care of the home like it is their own, because in a real way it is (or at least soon will be!) That means you won't get called at 3 a.m. to unclog a toilet or to unlock a door.

" I'll never forget the first time I was called out of bed in the middle of the night to take care of a property of mine. My renter had called about an "emergency" and I rushed right over. It turned out that it could have waited weeks (or at least until the next morning.) I've learned from those days. Now I use Purchase Option techniques to turn my properties into hands-off investments."

—PETER CONTI

You also get the best aspects of having a buyer from a tenant-buyer. They will pay you a substantial up-front payment (called an "option payment".) This payment is yours to keep even if they decide not to purchase the house. And because you are setting up the sale of the home at some future date, your tenant-buyer will pay you the future value of the home. Therefore you can pay the seller full price for his home and still make a healthy profit selling it to your tenant-buyer a few years down the road after it has appreciated in value!

In this section you'll learn:
- Exactly how you benefit from finding a tenant-buyer rather than an ordinary tenant or buyer
- The 12 steps you need to take to find your tenant-buyer once you get a property under contract
- How to get tenant-buyers to call you begging to buy your property (and what to say to them when they do call)
- How to make the "rent-to-own" concept seem irresistible to tenant-buyers
- How to create a ready reserve of tenant-buyers so that on future deals, you can make your money faster and with less effort
- How to show your property for maximum effect
- Everyone's biggest fear: "What happens if your tenant-buyer doesn't buy the property?" and why this means you're going to make even more money in the end

Section Five:
7 Fun, Easy Ways to Make Up to an Extra $100,000 This Year Investing in Real Estate

Once you thoroughly understand the basic structure of a Purchase Option deal, we will then explore all the alternatives you have when you put a Purchase Option deal into action.

You'll learn how to combine the best of the tried and true methods of the past with cutting edge techniques, resulting in the safest, most powerful investment strategies available.

One of the biggest benefits you get by using Purchase Option techniques is the wide variety of strategies you can call upon to close more deals, help more sellers, and make more money.

At the heart of these seven powerful Purchase Option techniques is one main theme: maximum profits with minimum effort and risk. It is that simple. In order for you to be a successful investor, you have to learn how to leverage your investment of time and money for maximum payoff and minimum risk.

In this section you'll learn:
- Three major benefits to Purchase Option techniques and how these techniques stack up, one versus the other in terms of profitability, effort, and risk
- Seven powerful Purchase Option techniques with enough punch to help you earn an extra $100,000 this year investing in real estate
- How to use "owner carry" financing to move into a deal with nothing down

24

- How to "flip" your Purchase Option contracts for quick-cash—now
- How to pull an extra $10,000 out of an otherwise "ordinary" deal
- Your last resort! How to turn a reluctant seller into your willing and eager partner
- How a former auto mechanic made $249,970.00 in four months—and how you can too

Section Six:
Putting It All Into Action:
Case Studies of How Our Students Put Together
Their Deals (And How You Can Too!)

In this section, you'll be able to study several real life case studies we've done with our students. You will learn exactly how Purchase Option deals are put together and how you can create deals too.

You'll see exactly how we found our motivated sellers. You'll understand the exact steps we used to lock up the deals. Finally, in some of the case studies you'll even hear where we found our tenant-buyers and how we received several thousand dollars more out of the deal than the average investor would.

This is your chance to go behind the scenes and walk step-by-step through several real deals from start to finish. You'll even hear from the students who made these deals about what they learned from the experience, what they would have done differently if they could go back, and how much money they actually made on each deal.

Section Seven:
Unlimited Wealth & Beyond

In the final section of the book, you are going to be amazed by a powerful new way to look at wealth. You'll learn why you are meant to be wealthy and how to unlock the financial genius inside of you.

With all this talk about money, in Beyond Unlimited Wealth you'll discover all the other aspects of wealth that are so much more important than just money. This will serve to heighten your enjoyment of the new wealth that you'll soon find pouring into your life.

About the Authors

Mechanic to Millionaire

I started out as an auto mechanic because that's what I had always been good at. Coming from a family of seven kids, I wasn't expected to amount to much. And for many years I bought into this concept of myself. Yet even during these times, a part of me hungered for more. All the time I was working for $5.00 an hour as a mechanic, I paid attention to what successful people were doing. Again and again I heard stories about people, who despite starting out with humble beginnings, were able to create great wealth in real estate.

Sometimes things need to get bad enough for you before you decide to make a change. For me, this point came when I was working in an auto repair shop. It was winter and the owner had the heat turned down. He was trying to save money. It was so cold that I remember my fingers were so numb I could barely even work.

I looked over as the shop foreman came out of the office with a big, hot, steaming cup of coffee. It looked so good I grabbed a coffee mug out of my toolbox and went into the office. After finding the coffeepot, I poured myself a nice warm mug of coffee and then wrapped my hands around it to warm them up more than anything.

Just as I was walking back to work, the owner came out of his office, looked at me said, "Peter, that coffee is for customers only!" I felt about two inches tall. But as bad as that felt, it was a great moment for me. I decided right then and there that I was never going to be dependent on

28

someone else again for my livelihood. Never again would anyone have that kind of power over my financial life. I thank God things got that bad because if they hadn't, I might never have committed to changing my life.

I had always known that real estate was a great way to create both wealth and freedom. So I finally took the leap and began my investing career. In the beginning, I scrimped and saved and bought every property I could. At the same time, I studied every book and tape program I could find. I went to every seminar I could afford. I continuously invested in myself and in my real estate knowledge base. Every technique and strategy I learned and applied paid me back 1,000 times over.

I remember my first fixer-upper property. It was a broken down 3-bedroom house in a working class neighborhood. The windows were all broken, and the roof leaked so badly that the kitchen ceiling had fallen in. I had picked it up cheap and had even gotten the owner to carry the financing.

When I added up all the repairs I thought the house would need, I got scared. What if I couldn't make more than it would cost me to fix up the house? It really needed a lot of work! In the end, I made a mistake. I sold out to another investor for $1,500. I felt good about this until I learned he had made about $30,000 on the deal.

If I had only been willing to admit that I needed some help, I could have found someone who had more experience than I did. Even if I had traded half of the profits in the deal in exchange for a mentor's expertise and guidance, I would have made $15,000 — 10 times more money!

My next major hurdle came, as my real estate portfolio grew too large. I soon began to realize that with each new property that I took on, more problems and responsibilities appeared.

All my tenants were looking to me and my company to give care and attention to their homes. In addition, a few undesirable tenants left me with a bad taste in my mouth. I had to work so hard just to keep all of my properties running smoothly.

I found that it wasn't too long before I moved from being a real estate investor into a property manager. The problem was that I was so caught up in the day to day management of my properties, that I wasn't out there buying more!

Even when I got to the point where I hired other people to do the fix-up work for me, I still spent most of my time overseeing their work and dealing with tenants. I was stuck in a spot that many investors, who try to make it using traditional real estate investing methods, find themselves.

I looked back over a two-year period and realized that I hadn't bought a single property in that time. My investing career had come to a standstill! I knew at that point that there had to be a better way. I spent several years looking for a smarter way to invest. Ultimately, this system was born out of my frustration with traditional real estate methods. It has come to be called Purchase Option investing.

The Purchase Option system has done away with the need to deal with tenants and toilets. You'll even be able to work the system part-time and still make big money. You'll discover, as many of my students and I have, that not only will you be making more money, but you'll be creating a lifestyle where you have the freedom to spend time with your family doing the things you want to do.

Many wealth seekers so often overlook this aspect. They realize after it's too late that they've taken a wrong turn. They forget that true wealth is living a balanced life... money, financial independence, free time, loving relationships, great health, and the ability to find your spiritual self.

Can you imagine waking up each day and deciding right then what you want to do that day? No more alarm clocks, no more dealing with your boss, no more rush hour traffic. Just time to pursue the life you've always wanted to live, and the time to go after your dreams. This life is waiting for you right now. I've helped thousands of people learn to create wealth through real estate. Let me show you the way...

—PETER CONTI

How an Ex-Olympic Level Athlete Became an Expert Real Estate Investor (And How You Can Too!)

I can remember my introduction to real estate. I had just retired from playing Olympic level hockey because of an injury. My background was in marketing and Peter hired me as a consultant. He wanted me to take all the cutting edge marketing ideas I had learned over the years and apply them to real estate. He wanted to make it easier for his students to make more money—faster—by getting motivated buyers and sellers to call his students and himself begging them to buy or sell.

Well, I spent the better part of a year helping put this powerful system in place and collected a hefty check for my work. But when I saw the even bigger dollars Peter and his students were making using his strategies, and combined them with my marketing plan, it hit me like a ton of bricks! I was making the biggest business mistake of my life.

Right there and then I made the decision to put real estate to work as my vehicle to financial freedom. It took some hard work, but with Peter's help and expertise I put his powerful Purchase Option tactics and techniques into action. One year later, I knew I would never have to worry about money again.

That's how powerful the ideas in this book are, and that is what they can do for you. They will give you the freedom to do what you want, when you want, where you want, and with whom you want.

Anyone can take a hold of the ideas in this book and put them into action for themselves. You can do it now! You just need to keep an open mind, take action on what you are learning, and commit to your lifelong real estate education. Remember, the more you learn—the more you earn!

The Purchase Option system is different from everything else out there. It incorporates all the benefits of traditional real estate—like cash flow, equity build-up, appreciation—while at the same time minimizing risk and rescuing you from the landlord trap of tenants and toilets. But don't take my word for it...find out for yourself! Pour over every word in this book, analyze every case study and test out each strategy. In the end, you will discover, as I did, that Purchase Option investing is the safest, fastest, and simplest road to wealth.

—DAVID FINKEL

"It is not because things are difficult that we do not dare; it is because we do not dare that they are difficult."

—SENECA

Section One:

How to Create Multiple Streams of Income

Buying Homes In Nice Areas With Nothing Down!

It is time to learn how you can enjoy all the benefits of owning real estate with none of the risks or hassles that traditionally come along with it. Purchase Option investing will give you multiple streams of monthly cash flow, quick-cash opportunities, and long-term wealth.

You will be creating multiple streams of income in two ways. First, each property you control will give you three main profit centers: up-front money, monthly cash flow, and property appreciation. Second, you will be creating multiple streams of income by intelligently structuring your deals so that you can earn big profits from several properties at the same time. This diversification will not only make you wealthier, but will also give you security and peace of mind.

Traditional Investing

So, let's start from the beginning. What does it mean to buy an investment property the traditional way?

You find a property, pay a substantial down payment, and finance the balance through a mortgage lender. Of course, to buy a property the traditional way, you need three things: a large down payment, strong credit, and a healthy monthly income.

Let's take a moment to look closer at these three areas in turn.

1) Large Down Payment:

When you are buying an investment property the traditional way, most lenders are going to require you to put between 20-30 percent down before they will finance your new property. Also, investment interest rates are generally HIGHER than interest rates for properties in which you plan to live. This, of course, will eat into your monthly cash flow.

2) Strong Credit:

Without an established credit history, you can forget about getting a loan on most investment properties.

3) Healthy Monthly Income:

The third and final requirement for buying a property the traditional way is a steady source of monthly income. Of course, in the world of mortgage lenders, this means that you have been with your employer for several years and earn enough to pay the monthly payments in the event you can't find a renter for your property. If you're self-employed, things just got a lot tougher for you. If you don't have at least two years of tax returns and bank statements to support your application, you won't be getting that investment loan.

Let's just say you have all three of these requirements. What do you do now? If you are investing the traditional way, you find a renter for your property and manage it for the next 30 years until you own it free and clear. Of course, along the way, you deal with the showings, rent collection, maintenance, renter evictions, and all the other rental property joys.

Still, in the long run, you will end up building a great deal of long-term equity in your property, both from paying down the loan over the 30 years and also from the property's appreciation over time. If you did nothing more than buy 5-10 properties, and then manage them for the next thirty years, you would become a millionaire. It is a sure road to wealth.

Yet when faced with these realities, traditional real estate investing scares many investors away. Why? Because *traditional* investing techniques have four major pitfalls.

The Four Pitfalls of Traditional Real Estate Investing

Pitfall #1: Need for a large down payment

Remember that requirement to buy an investment property the traditional way? 20-30% down!

Of course, as soon as you put a large down payment into a deal, you fall prey to the second pitfall of traditional real estate.

Pitfall #2: High risk

The more money you have in a deal, the greater your risk in that transaction. Obviously, if you have $30,000 into a property, you can't just walk away from the deal if things don't go well. You are tied to that deal. In investing, the best course of action is to keep your up-front investment as low as possible. If you are able to keep your up-front investment at zero, then your effective risk is zero too! (Or, as close to zero as possible in today's world.)

Pitfall #3: Negative cash flow

Properties have appreciated in value over 6.5% per year in the U.S. over the last 50 years. While property values have shot up, rental rates just have not kept pace. For most investors, this means in the first five to ten years of owning a rental property, they have to deal with negative cash flow.

Homes in the lower income areas can be rented for positive cash flows, but then investors have to deal with the management headaches associated with these types of homes. In the past, when you wanted to invest in middle and upper income homes, you had little choice but to cover the negative monthly cash flow yourself in the early years, in order to enjoy the big payoff in the end. But now it doesn't have to be that way.

In this book, you are going to learn how you can control beautiful homes in nice areas and have multiple streams of *positive* cash flow right from the very start!

Pitfall #4: The landlord trap

For every investor who acquires a large number of properties, there is a point at which he falls prey to the "landlord trap." At this point, the investor is so busy maintaining and managing what he already has, that he doesn't have the time to go out and buy more properties.

Depending on how well an investor manages his portfolio, he might hit this barrier at 20 units, or he may make it all the way to several hundred units. Still, at some point, he will hit it and fall into the landlord trap.

The Pen Versus the Hammer

As an investor, you make your money by buying and selling properties. When you use your pen to write an agreement to buy or sell a property, you are making vast sums of money. But when you fall prey to the landlord trap and exchange your pen for a hammer or a paintbrush, your income plummets.

Even if you don't do the fix-up and management work yourself, you still have to hire someone else to do it. You will be spending your precious time overseeing the process, making sure the work is done right. Your income will take a big hit. Smart investors understand they make their biggest profits as investors, not as property managers.

Here, you have the four pitfalls of traditional real estate investing. With all these obstacles, it's no wonder that so many people get stuck not knowing how to get started investing in real estate. They know it's a good thing. They have seen many people make their fortunes investing in properties. But in the past, these obstacles have made it tough for them to get started.

Not any longer! It's time for you to learn how to sidestep these pitfalls as you get started buying homes in nice areas with nothing down.

If you're like us, you probably want to make that money *faster*, and avoid all the headaches that come from dealing with tenants and toilets. That's why we created the Purchase Option system. We looked at all the benefits of owning real estate, as well as the pitfalls. Then, we created a way to enjoy the three most important benefits of owning real estate *and* at the same time avoid the four major pitfalls of traditional real estate investing. The resulting system has been the vehicle for thousands of people to create *massive* bank accounts over the past few years.

With all these obstacles to investing in real estate, is it any wonder that you've had trouble getting started in the past? But that's all in the past! Now you are armed with the most powerful, easiest and safest real estate investment strategy ever developed.

The Three Big Benefits of Purchase Option Investing

Purchase Option investing lets you realize the three biggest benefits of owning investment properties:

1) Multiple Streams of Monthly Cash Flow

When you own an investment property, each month you collect rent and pay out specific expenses. The money you have left over creates your cash flow—i.e. money you have left over for yourself. The best part about Purchase Option investing is that it allows you to build up bigger streams of monthly cash flow than traditional real estate investing. In fact, you are going to learn how to rent out your properties for MORE than the going market rent. And each year your residual income from cash flow will increase as you both raise your rents and take control of more properties. Each new property you add to your growing portfolio is an additional stream of monthly income—giving you more spendable cash and diversifying your risk over several properties.

41

2) Quick-Cash

As an investor, your biggest payday comes from holding onto your investment property long enough for its value to appreciate by thousands of dollars. This takes time though. Using the Purchase Option system, you are able to cash out of deals by selling your interest in a property to another party. This is known as "flipping" your deal. You are going to learn how you can flip your deals and the two best people you can flip them to.

3) Long-Term Wealth Building

Obviously, real estate goes up in value over time. You already know that. It is the greatest wealth-builder ever created. You are going to learn how to lock up an investment property with little or no up-front money, then ride the appreciation curve, creating long-term financial freedom. Also, since you will be locking up many properties at below market prices, you will be creating thousands of dollars in instant equity in your properties.

Purchase Option Simplified

Have you ever seen a "rent to own" store? Did you know that you could walk into that store and buy a brand new big screen TV? All you need to do is make nice, easy monthly payments and in a few years, you will own that TV. Of course, in the long run, you will end up paying between two and three times more for that TV than if you paid cash up front.

How about the latest way of getting a new car—leasing to own. You simply make a small down payment and then each month you make an easy lease payment. At the end of your lease period (usually three or five years), you have the option to buy that car for X dollars more. Or, you can simply hand back the keys and go find another car, if you choose. Of course, if you buy the car on these "lease to own" plans, you will end up paying more than if you had purchased it for all cash up front.

Why would people pay more for something on a "rent to own" basis? Because they are paying a premium for the easy financing with which they are then able to own that item. And the best part for you is that you can do the exact same thing with real estate!

Just by controlling a property and changing the terms with which you make it available to a new buyer, you instantly increase the value of that property. This sentence needs repeating because it is crucial to your bank account.

Just by controlling a property and changing the terms with which you make it available to a new buyer, you instantly increase the value of that property.

You are going to be using the "rent to own" concept (which has been around for many years) in a new way—with real estate. How?

You are going to be a matchmaker, linking up a motivated seller and a hungry tenant-buyer. And by helping both these people get what they want, you are going to get paid handsomely for your efforts.

A motivated seller is a property owner whose sole aim in life at that moment is to get rid of his property. There are seven main reasons motivated sellers sell which you will be learning shortly. However, for the moment, what is important is that you understand that when you find and put together a deal with a motivated seller, you are helping them win. Remember, for them, the property is a problem, whether it's because of debt or distance, and they need your help in fashioning a win-win solution.

Your hungry tenant-buyer is someone who desperately wants to own his or her own home, but for one reason or another, can't qualify to buy a home the traditional way. Remember those three things you need to buy a home traditionally: large down payment, good credit, and high monthly income? Well, your tenant-buyer is someone who is lacking in one of these key areas.

For example, your tenant-buyer may be someone who had a bankruptcy five years ago. As you may know, it takes seven years for that to clear off his credit record. You are able to help him come into your property as a tenant-buyer—renting to own the property. After two or three years, that bankruptcy clears off his credit record and your tenant-buyer can now qualify for a new loan and cash you out of the property.

Let's walk through a simplified example of what we are talking about.

Purchase Option: The Overview

There are three steps to any Purchase Option deal. Step one is to find a motivated seller. Step two is to find out exactly what the seller's needs are and craft a win-win solution to meet those needs while creating a profit for yourself. Step three is for you to find an end buyer for the property— your tenant-buyer.

Let's start with **step one**—finding your motivated seller and creating a win-win solution to his real estate problem.

Randy is a motivated seller. He was offered a new job four months ago in a new city. The job is a great career move, with an increase in pay and prestige. The problem for Randy is that he hasn't been able to sell his house yet. He tried listing it with a realtor for three months and it just wouldn't sell. Now he is faced with moving in just three weeks.

His options are either to slash the price of the house for a quick sale, something he is hesitant to do, or he can rent it out until he can find a buyer. (But then he would have to either manage the property and renter *long distance* or hire a *property manager* and pay them to manage the property—typically 10% of the monthly rent.)

That's where you come in. As a Purchase Option investor, you are able to help solve Randy's problem with **step two**—you come in and agree to rent out Randy's house for six years for the amount of his payments. At the same time, you agree upon a price at which you can buy the house at any time you choose over that six-year period. (This is called a "lease option" or a "lease purchase" and it is the foundational strategy of the Purchase Option system. You will learn about seven other Purchase Option strategies later in this book.)

Take a moment to look over Chart 1 on page 46 and you'll see exactly what you have done.

Randy's payments on the house are $1,400 a month (this includes principle, interest, taxes, and insurance.) You will cover this amount so that Randy will have no costs associated with his property over the period in which you control it before you purchase it. (You'll learn how you will deal with the maintenance later.)

As for the price, to show you how you can "pay" the seller full price and still make money for yourself, you have agreed to pay the seller full market value for the property. In this case, it is $200,000.

With Purchase Option investing, you can offer the seller full price and still make a huge profit for yourself. Obviously, if you are a good negotiator and are able to bring that price down, then you will end up making even more money. So, you are locking in the price at today's value (or less) for a long period of time. As that property appreciates, you will capture the future appreciation as one of your profit centers in each deal.

What Does It Take Up-Front?

Now, if you are like the students we work with across the country, you will probably be able to lock-up the property without giving the seller any up-front money. (Actually, you will give the seller $1 up-front as "legal consideration" to make your agreement binding.)

On the original San Diego Challenge, we were able to lock up over $1.5 million dollars worth of real estate with only $37 in up-front money! We locked-up ten separate properties ranging in value from $60,000 to $500,000 with only $37. And if we can do it, so can you!

You, The Investor

Motivated Seller   Hungry Tenant-Buyer

$1,400 | Rent |

$200,000 | Price |

6 Years | Term |

$2,000 | Pymt |

Chart 1

You, The investor, are leasing out property with the option to purchase. This is one of the powerful Purchase Option techniques.

Just like you would imagine, if you are able to give the seller up-front money, then you are able to close more deals. In this example, you are going to give the seller $2,000.

Wait a second, you say… You haven't got $2,000! Just hang in there because in a moment, you are going to learn where you are going to find this money. (And here's a hint for you—*it won't be from your wallet!*)

Let's get clear on exactly what you and Randy have agreed upon. You have agreed to rent out the property for six years for the amount of the monthly payments ($1,400.) You have also agreed on a price (in this case full market value of $200,00) at which you can buy the property at any point over the next six years. In essence, you have negotiated a lease with the option to buy. (Note: we are using a sales price of $200,000—full market value—in order to show you how you can offer full price and still build in a healthy profit for yourself. Obviously if you are able to negotiate the price lower, you will make even more money.)

As for the $2,000 of up-front money, you are going to tell your motivated seller, "Randy, I will give you the $2,000 as soon as I take occupancy of the property or find someone to occupy the property."

You'll see in just a moment why it is critical for you to add this part into your agreement, because it will be essential in your funding of this deal.

The Secret of Nothing-Down Deals

Here is the secret to doing nothing-down deals:

Nothing down does *not* mean "nothing" to the seller. Nothing down means none of *your* money goes to the seller.

48

The distinction is critical. Your motivated seller may get money up-front… it just won't be your money!

Now you're ready to move to **step three**—finding your hungry tenant-buyer. In this case, your tenant-buyers are the Smiths. The Smiths are a middle-aged couple who started their own business last year. They have good credit. However, because they don't have two or three years of tax returns and bank account records showing the income they have been generating from their business to support their loan application, they can't get a loan the traditional way… yet. (Remember, they have been in business less than one year.)

You are able to help the Smiths by letting them "rent to own" the house. This means that the Smiths will rent out the property from you with a price you have set in advance. (Take a close look at Chart 2 on page 49 to see exactly how these numbers fit into place.)

In this example, the Smiths are going to rent the property from you for three years. (There is a specific reason you always want a longer term with your motivated seller than with your tenant-buyer that you'll soon learn.) The market rent in the area is $1,700. The Smiths are coming into the property on a rent to own basis, so they willingly pay you above-market rent! In this case, they pay you $1,800 for rent.

You also agree with the Smiths on a price at which they can purchase the property at any point over the next three years. Because you want this to be a win for the Smiths too, you set the price at less than the house will be worth in three years.

If the house appreciates at just 7 percent, then in one year it will be worth $214,000. We are leaving the money-making effects of compounding out of the equation to keep the

You, The Investor

Motivated Seller		Hungry Tenant-Buyer
$1,400	**Rent**	**$1,800**
$200,000	**Price**	**$230,000**
6 Years	**Term**	**3 Years**
$2,000	**Pymt**	**$10,000**

Chart 2

You have found your Tenant-Buyer and collected $10,000 from them as an up-front "option" payment.

concept simple. After three years, the house will be worth $242,000. You are going to let the Smiths have a purchase price of just $230,000! You can feel good that you are giving them a tremendous value.

Because of this value you are giving the Smiths, they will pay you 3-5% of the value of the property as an up-front payment (technically called an "option payment.") In this case, you collect $10,000 from the Smiths up-front as their option payment on the property. This money gets credited off the purchase price when the Smiths buy. And in the event they choose not to buy the house, it is non-refundable.

After a year or two, the Smiths will be able to get a new loan from their mortgage lender and cash out both you and the motivated seller, Randy. In essence, that's how the system works.

How You Fund Your Deals Up Front

Remember the $2,000 you owe Randy, the motivated seller? Where do you think you are going to get it? That's exactly right! You are going to take the $10,000 cashiers check you collect from the Smiths, deposit it, and give $2,000 of it to Randy. What happens to the remaining $8,000? You get to keep it!

You might think this is a nothing-down deal, but it's not. It's better than that. This is a nothing-down deal with an $8,000 rebate!

Let's add up your profits (See Chart 3 on page 51) Each month you are earning $400 in cash flow. Over 36 months that adds up to $14,400. You are buying the house for $200,000 and the Smiths are paying you $230,000. So you

You, The Investor

Motivated Seller

	$400/month	
$1,400	**Rent**	**$1,800**
	$30,000	
$200,000	**Price**	**$230,000**
6 Years	**Term**	**3 Years**
$2,000	**Pymt**	**$10,000**

Chart 3

36 months x $400/month = $14,400
Plus spread in prices   = $30,000

$44,400

make an additional $30,000 from the spread in the prices.

All totaled, you earned $44,400 from this Purchase Option deal. Congratulations!

Let's look at some ways to make this deal even better for you.

How to Lower Your Effective Risk to Zero

Imagine you were buying an investment property the traditional way. You have narrowed down your choice to three houses located on the same block.

Right now you need to choose: Do you want to buy house number one, house number two, or house number three? Circle the house you choose now.

You bought this house the traditional way, so you now have to sit back and hope. You hope that you will be able to find a renter. You hope that you will be able to rent it out for more than your payment. You hope that you won't have any major repairs to make. You hope for a lot of things. And then you wait and see how you did over time.

Are you ready to find out how you did?

House number one was a small profit: $17,200. House number two was a disaster: a $900 loss. However, house number three paid off handsomely: $44,400.

That's traditional real estate investing. You buy your properties and find out how you did afterward.

The biggest difference with Purchase Option investing is that you know how you are going to do *before* you move ahead with the deal.

If you were able to see into the future and see how each of our three sample houses were going to turn out, which house would you have chosen to buy? You would have chosen house number three, wouldn't you? With Purchase Option investing, that is exactly what you are able to do. You will know up front how the deal will turn out for you.

How can you do this? You will use a "subject to" clause, which states that your agreement with the motivated seller is "subject to" you finding a qualified resident to occupy the property. In other words, your agreement is "subject to" you finding a qualified tenant-buyer. If you don't find your tenant-buyer, then you don't move ahead with the deal.

What you do when setting up a Purchase Option deal is to have both halves of the transaction complete before you ever fully commit to the deal. You find your motivated seller and lock up the property. Then you quickly go out and find your tenant-buyer. Then, and only then, do you fully commit to moving ahead with the deal.

In our example, at the point when your tenant-buyers, the Smiths, give you a check for $10,000 and another check for the first month's rent of $1,800, do you think you would feel confident enough to move ahead with the deal? Of course you would.

CAUTION! When you use such a powerful "subject to" clause, you need to be respectful of the seller. You need to let them know right away if you are having any problems finding your tenant-buyers—within two to three weeks. Under no circumstances would you ever want to tie up a seller's property for several months and then tell them that you cannot find your tenant-buyer. That would be both unfair and wrong.

How to Sidestep The Landlord Trap

Unless you have a way to get out of the hassle of the day to day management of a property, you are still going to run into the landlord trap. Let's be honest, you are investing in real estate in order to create a better lifestyle, right? So if you are responsible for managing each property and looking after the maintenance, then it doesn't matter how much money you are making, you still will not have the freedom and quality of life you are after.

Here is a way you can safely sidestep the landlord trap and escape the headaches and hassles of tenants and toilets.

When you are talking with the motivated seller, you will say to them, "Mr. Seller, to make this a real win for you, would you like me to take care of the day-to-day maintenance on the property? Why don't I take care of the first $200 of maintenance in any one month? That should take care of 98 percent of the problems. Would that work for you?"

Of course, the seller will be thrilled that you will be taking over the day-to-day upkeep on the property.

But wait a minute, you say, how does that get you out of the landlord trap? Next you go meet with your tenant-buyer. You tell your tenant-buyer, "Mr. Tenant-buyer, you're coming into this property as if you are the future owner. And we expect that you would treat the place as if you did in fact own it. Of course this means that you are going to be responsible for the maintenance on the property. But to make it a win for you and so that you know that you won't have any major repairs that you are responsible for, let's put a limit on it—the first $200 in any one month."

See how easy it was for you to sidestep the landlord trap? If a repair happens and it costs over $200, who is responsible for it? That's right, the seller is responsible. If a repair happens that is less than $200, who is responsible for it? That's right, your tenant-buyer. What are you left responsible for? Nothing! You get to sit in the middle, making money without the headaches and hassles of traditional real estate.

Of course, you do have specific responsibilities. Each month you have to collect a check, deposit a check, and write a check. The beauty of the system is that once you have set up a property correctly and you collect a chunk of money up front, you have a hands-off residual stream of income that flows to you each and every month. Then at the end of a period of time, you get a flood of money when your tenant-buyer gets his own loan on the property, cashing both you and the motivated seller out of the deal.

Creating Multiple Streams of Income

Let's say it took you an entire year to find and put together your first Purchase Option deal. (We have students who are averaging one a month working just a few hours a day in their spare time.) After a year of part-time effort, you have your first deal set up. You collected a big chunk up front as the option payment. Each month you are earning a residual stream of income from the property, and you will collect a huge chunk of money down the line when your tenant-buyer gets new financing and purchases the property.

The next year, you go out and look for more deals. By now, you are much better at it and you find two deals. Again, once you set up each deal, it's a hands-off investment pumping residual streams of monthly cash flow into your bank account. In year three, you find four properties in your spare time and set them up. You keep doing more and more deals as your expertise increases. The only limit is your own ambition.

Each deal is an independent money-making machine for you. It gives you cash up front, a monthly stream of cash flow, and a final payday when your tenant-buyer buys. This is how you create multiple streams of income buying homes in nice areas with nothing down.

Most People's Biggest Fear
(And why it means you'll probably end up making twice as much money!)

Without question, the biggest fear new Purchase Option investors have is: *What happens if my tenant-buyer doesn't exercise their option and buy the property?* Remember, the tenant-buyer has the option to buy the property, not the obligation to buy.

We can certainly understand the concern. After all, it sure seems that if the tenant-buyer doesn't buy, then we are going to lose out. This just isn't so. Not only are you still in a very secure position, but if your tenant-buyer doesn't buy, you're probably going to make a whole lot *more* money—often twice as much!

Here's why. First, if your tenant-buyer decides not to buy, what happens to their non-refundable option payment? That's right, *you get to keep it.* Plus, since the house was a "rent to own" home, you probably have been enjoying a **healthy cash flow** from the **above-market rents** they have been paying you. You get to keep the monthly streams of cash flow you have been collecting. Not a bad situation considering the tenant-buyer has been taking care of the property because they had planned to buy it.

Remember that you learned to arrange your lease with the motivated seller for a LONGER period than you do with your tenant-buyer. You will have at least one more year (usually more) to find a new tenant-buyer and collect another up front option payment. **Bonus—Since the property has probably appreciated in value, you can get a larger option payment, higher rent, and charge a higher sales price!**

Let's make this point absolutely clear by going back to our earlier example. You signed a Purchase Option agreement with Randy, your motivated seller, for a maximum term of six years. Your purchase price was $200,000, and your monthly rent was $1,400.

You found your tenant-buyers, the Smiths, who pay you $1,800 a month in rent, gave you $10,000 up front as their option payment, and agreed to the $230,000 price. Their term was three years.

Three years later the Smiths decide not to exercise their option (i.e., they decide not to buy the house.) What happens next?

You keep the $14,400 from monthly cash flow, and the $10,000 option payment. (Remember that you have already given $2,000 of the option payment to your motivated seller, Randy.) Then, you go out and find a second tenant-buyer. (See Chart 4 on page 59)

The total sum that you have earned is $22,400 from a property your first tenant-buyer didn't buy.

Remember, if the property had only appreciated by 7% per year for each of the three years of the term, it is now worth $242,000! So of course, you collect a slightly larger option payment from your second tenant-buyer and you charge a slightly higher monthly rent. (Doesn't it make sense that the rent should increase after three years?) You also set the purchase price at a much higher value, between $260,000 and $270,000.

To make sure you have the concept, let's say you wanted to find your second tenant-buyer fast. So you advertised the property and didn't raise the rent. You charged only $1,800 a month in rent, which by now was below market rent. And

You, The Investor

Motivated Seller

$1,400	**Rent**	**$1,800**

$200,000	**Price**	**value: $284,000**

6 Years	**Term**	

$2,000	**Pymt**	

Total Profits:

Collected from Tenant-Buyer #1

36 months x $400/month	+ $14,400
Up-front Option Payment	+ $10,000
Less Money Given to Seller	– $ 2,000
	=$22,400

Collected from Tenant-Buyer #2

36 months x $400/month	+ $14,400
Up-front Option Payment	+ $ 8,000
	= $22,400

Total Profits Before You Sell = $44,800

Total Profits After You Sell Property for $230,000 = $74,800

Chart 4

you only collected another $8,000 of option money up-front from your tenant buyer. Then you sit back and collect those fat monthly checks from the property.

You get to enjoy a positive cash-flow of $400 a month for another three years and ride the appreciation curve up on an asset you do not own, haven't signed personally on a loan for, and have zero maintenance responsibilities for. How's that for a great deal?

You might be wondering, what happens if your second tenant-buyer decides not to buy as well? Again, this is still OK for you. Here's why: You have enjoyed a total of six years of positive cash flow and collected over $16,000 of option money. You are well ahead of the game. At this point, you have earned $44,800 from the property.

The worst case scenario is for you to tell the owner of the property that you do not want to buy the property. Remember that you also had the option to purchase the property, not the obligation.

You could simply give the home back to the original owner. In that case, you would have profited by the monthly cash flow and the two option payments. The money made is not bad for such a hands-off investment.

As for the original owner, Randy, he will put you on his Christmas card list for the rest of his life! Why? Well, instead of buying the house for $200,000, you gave him back a property that is worth $284,000 that you looked after for the past six years. Do you think Randy is going to mind that you are giving him back $84,000 in equity? Of course not!

Before you do that though, let me suggest an alternate game plan for you. You have a $284,000 house that you can

61

buy for $200,000. Following the Purchase Option system, you have a "90 Day Notification Clause" in your agreement with your tenant-buyer. This clause says that your tenant-buyer has to give you a minimum of 90 days notice that they want to buy the house. If the second tenant-buyer does not buy, this clause gives you a full three months notice to sell the property to another buyer.

At this point, you can list the house with a Realtor and price it for a quick sale. Or you can sell it yourself. If you want a quick sale, then you can use an ad like this:

"DESPERATE! MUST SELL!
Take my $284,000 house for only
$230,000. Must close within 14 days.
Certified funds only. Call 222-3333"

Even if you were to discount the property by over $50,000 for an instant sale, you would make an additional $30,000. When you add this to your $44,800, it equals $74,800—almost twice what you would have made if your first tenant-buyers, the Smiths, had purchased the property!

So you see, if your tenant-buyer buys... you win. If your tenant-buyer doesn't buy... you win bigger! That's the power of Purchase Option investing. You cash in on the three big benefits of owning property without the risks of traditional real estate investing.

Throughout this book, you will be learning how to complete all three steps in a Purchase Option deal: finding your motivated seller, locking up the property, and finding your tenant-buyer.

It is time to learn the first step—finding your motivated seller. You will learn the inside secrets of finding flexible sellers, which is the master key that will unlock the door to success in real estate. Let's continue together!

"Some will, some won't,
so what? Next!"

—MARK VICTOR HANSON

Section Two:

How to Find
Motivated Sellers

A motivated seller is a property owner whose sole aim in life at the time you are talking with him is to get rid of his piece of property.

I've been a motivated seller before. I was so down on my luck at one point in my life that I didn't have enough money to pay my bills. I called up a real estate agent who was a friend of mine and said, "Jimmy, I don't care how you do it, but I need you to sell my house in the next two weeks."

Jimmy sold my house. He even found a buyer before the two weeks were up. He sold it for $500 less than I had paid for it six years earlier. Despite this loss, I was happy to get away from the property because it was like a lead anchor dragging me down.

I've also been on the other side of the table as well. One time a motivated seller paid me $10,000 at closing to buy his 12-unit apartment building. His name was Clay. He was going through some relationship troubles and wanted out.

I met up with Clay several years later and he said to me, "Peter, I'm so glad that you bought that building from me."

"Oh really?" I said thinking about the $1,600 a month positive cash flow the property was making for me.

"Before you bought that building, I was worried night

66

and day. Thanks so much for helping me out Peter."

"No problem Clay," I said, realizing this was a business where you could help people out, and make a lot of money too.

—Peter Conti

The reality is that motivated sellers exist. They always have and they always will. In fact, in any marketplace, at any time, there are always a set percentage of sellers who are highly motivated to sell their properties.

Why? Because of the following fact:

Most motivated sellers are created by personal reasons, not economic reasons.

Market crashes in an entire area are rare. In most cases, motivated sellers are created by some personal situation unique to that individual. While this personal situation is unique to the seller, you need to understand that there are patterns that play out over and over. You will be able to concentrate your marketing efforts on these known pools of highly motivated sellers.

The Seven Reasons Why Motivated Sellers Sell

1. Relocation

When a seller is moving and can't sell his house, he is faced with potential double payments or with the prospects of managing his property as a long distance rental. When a homeowner gets into a situation where they have to transfer because of his work or move because of other reasons, the scene is set for a possible motivated seller. The owner will usually have a specific date on which he will be moving or leaving. The closer you are to that date, the more motivated the seller will be.

"I'm Moving Next Week!"

One of our students, Samantha, found a seller who owned a nice home that he had not been able to sell. The seller was leaving the country to go live in South America in six days! He was incredibly motivated.

He was thrilled when he realized that Samantha was able to help him out of his situation! Of course, Samantha was happy too, because this deal looked like it would result in $40,000 of profits.

—DAVID FINKEL

Finding motivated sellers is fun when you go after it with the right attitude. Ideally, you want to feel like sellers are chasing after you, not you chasing them.

A student had asked me to help him put together a deal with a seller of a home who had already moved out of state and was forced to make payments on two homes. When I called and talked with the seller, I asked him what he hoped I could do for him. I'll never forget the words he used to describe what he wanted from me, "I just want you to make the bleeding stop."

When you can help someone like that, you feel incredibly proud because you truly know you are out there helping people.

—DAVID FINKEL

2. Divorce and relationship problems

Many times a home can be an emotional anchor that ties

a person to a painful memory. When two people who are married or involved in a serious relationship decide to call it quits, it's not at all uncommon for a nice home to come up for sale... and quick. Divorce creates the need to sell a property for three reasons.

1) It costs too much for one person to live in the home by him or her self.
2) Dividing the assets is the easiest way to get a clean break in the relationship.
3) Emotions from the relationship are linked to the house, and the owners want a fresh start.

One of our students named John had gone through a divorce right before he came through one of our training sessions. While he was learning how to find motivated sellers, he realized that he and his former wife were motivated sellers!

We helped John put together a deal on his own house that allowed him to make an extra $20,000 over what he would have made if he had just sold the house quickly to get rid of it. But John didn't stop there. He used the Purchase Option techniques to buy his next house too!

—Peter Conti

There are many sellers out there working to put the pieces of their lives back together after the painful aftermath of a breakup. These people need your help to get out from the pressing reality of having to deal with their property.

[**Editor's note:** If you use this information for nothing other than to buy or sell your next house more intelligently, you will be repaid a hundred fold for your investment of time reading this book. You might very well save several thousand dollars on your purchase by finding a motivated seller to buy from.]

3. Financial difficulties

Debt and money troubles are a reality for many sellers. Given the choice between foreclosure and selling, many owners choose to sell. One group of homeowners who need your help are those who've managed to get behind in their payments. They could just be a month or two behind, or they could be much farther behind and face immediate foreclosure. Using Purchase Option techniques you are able to help these struggling sellers and earn a profit too.

I went out to meet with Tom, a motivated seller, who was faced with bankruptcy in less than two months. As I sat down and talked with Tom, it became clear that he wanted to figure out a way to keep from having a foreclosure on his credit record as well. We came up with a win-win solution. I signed up a six year lease option deal on the home that would not only save him from having a foreclosure, but would also mean a healthy profit for me. When I left him that day, Tom shook my hand and said thank you for helping him make the best of a tough situation.

—DAVID FINKEL

4. Tenant trouble

One of the best sources of motivated sellers are landlords who want out. There are three reasons they make great motivated sellers. First, they are already used to leasing out their property. This is the first half of a Purchase Option deal. Second, they are used to letting someone live in their property, controlling it, for just one month's security deposit. While this isn't nothing down, it is almost nothing down. Third, since the property was a rental and not their primary residence, chances are they won't need all their equity out of the property to immediately go buy another property.

"I'm just tired of tenants"

When James and I met Rick and Beverly, we were impressed by their home's appearance. Rick had spent the last year remodeling the entire property. You would never know it had been a rental for them.

Rick and Beverly wanted out of the rental business. They wanted to sell off all of their property and travel around the country in an RV. They had listed this home for six months with an asking price of $269,000, but it just hadn't sold.

James and I offered a five-year lease paying $1,130 a month, which covered their mortgage payments. We also got an option to buy the property for $250,000 at any time over the next five years.

Why would they agree to this when they had rented the property for $1600 a month (before they fixed it up?) Rick and Beverly were sick and tired of the rental business. They knew that James and I would be making at least $400 a month in cash flow. They just wanted to be done with this property so that they could retire from the rental business and travel around the country. That house is now worth over $300,000!

—PETER CONTI

71

5. Probate

Many people who inherit property don't want to have any involvement with the property. They just want to sell it. If they can't sell it themselves, then your creative offer just might be the best way out for them.

One of the untapped areas of investing is finding owners who have received a home through probate. Homes go into probate when a person dies and leaves their house to a relative.

Many people who inherit a property are willing to accept much less for the property than it is actually worth. After all, it was given to them. They didn't have to work hard to buy the house. And just like someone who has won the lottery becomes better at spending overnight, the new owner of a home received through probate is often willing to take less in order to turn a house into cash.

I got a call on an ad I had placed looking for motivated sellers. The seller who called me had inherited a large four-bedroom house a few years back when his father passed away. The seller needed some money right away because he needed to get his truck back from the auto company that had repossessed it. He was willing to do anything as long as it got him his truck back.

The house was worth $360,000 and the seller had over $150,000 worth of equity in the property. Over the phone he agreed to sell it to me for $280,000 paid as follows: $10,000 cash within 48 hours, with his remaining equity due within five years as a zero interest balloon note! Not only had he agreed to discount the price of the home by $80,000, but he was also going to carry back the financing of the home with no interest for five years!

Unfortunately for me, in the one and a half days before I went to meet with the seller he found someone else who bought the property from him for $330,000.

The moral of the story is clear. When you find a good deal, you need to move fast or you'll lose out!

—David Finkel

6. Downsizing to a smaller house

Faced with too much house, many sellers simply want to sell and find a more modest place to live. For example, the seller's children may have grown up and moved out. Then the seller is left with an empty nest which is much too large, and a little bit lonely.

Her name was Sylvia and she owned a beautiful, large home that she lived in by herself. The problem was that it was too large for her. Sylvia was nearing her mid-sixties and she found the upkeep on the home was too much for her. She wanted out so that she could find a smaller and more manageable place to live.

—DAVID FINKEL

7. Wanting a larger home

Growing families can stretch the seams of small houses which sparks the need for a larger place to live. Of course, for most people this means selling their old house.

Mary and Paul had three children with one more on the way. They lived in a cramped, three-bedroom, one-bath house. They had been trying to sell their home for a year with no success, when one of our students met them. She signed up a lease-purchase deal that would help them handle their property and buy a bigger house.

And the deal was structured to let our student turn a healthy profit on the deal.

—Peter Conti

You now know why motivated sellers sell. You also know what signs to be looking for when you are talking with a seller.

There are two criteria you must examine in your search for a motivated seller:

1. The seller's motivation
2. The seller's situation

Think about the "M" in motivated seller representing the seller's reasons for selling—her *motivation*. And the "S" stands for the seller's *situation*. You need to find a seller with both.

First you must dig to understand the seller's motivation for selling the property. Does the seller's motivation fit into one of the seven categories you just learned? When is their deadline for selling? What else have they tried and what alternatives do they have left? How open have they been ABOUT sharing their situation with you? All of these questions will help you determine if the seller has a *compelling* reason to sell.

Next you need to understand the seller's situation. As an investor, you need to find a seller who is either flexible on the price of the property or on the terms of the sale. If the seller needs full price and all cash at closing, it is almost impossible for you, as an investor, to make a profit on the home. Before a property becomes attractive for an all cash price to a savvy investor, the price needs to drop by 30-40 percent. While many investors aggressively negotiate with sellers on the price in the hopes of beating them down by these percentages, the Purchase Option system is designed to allow you to offer a higher price to the seller in exchange for flexible terms.

As a creative investor who wants to help people and make money, you are looking for a seller who has flexibility on the terms of the sale. You want someone who does not need all of their cash out of the property up front. Does the seller need her equity out of her home to go buy her next home? Or does she already own a second home? What would the seller do if she could not sell? If she would rent it out for a few years and then go to sell, she can potentially be flexible on the terms of sale.

"How will I know when I've found one?"

I was working with one of our students named Craig teaching him how to use Purchase Option to create the financial freedom he wanted for his family. Craig was making a lot of money in his job but he needed to make even more to be able to send his two sons through college.

We had set a joint goal of getting Craig into his first deal within the first 90 days. Actually, Craig wanted to get it sooner.

We had been working together for about 60 days when Craig called on the phone sounding frustrated. "Just what do these motivated sellers look like and when am I going to meet one?" he said.

"Craig," I said, "You'll know it when you meet one." You see, I've trained enough people to do this, and I know that if you follow the system, it's only a matter of time before you get your first deal.

"I've found him! I've found him!" Craig shouted a week later.

"Tell me more." I encouraged, getting curious now.

"I found a guy who wanted to give me $5,000 to take over his property!" Craig finally knew what it was like to be talking with a motivated seller.

That was Craig's first deal. He and his wife went on to do nine deals in their first 9 months using the Purchase Option system.

Several months later, Craig and his son came back to one of the intensive sessions I hold a few times each year to train my students.

I will never forget how moving it was to watch Craig's son stand in front of the group and say how thankful he was for real estate, the Purchase Option system, and his parents for making it possible for him to go to college. The thing that sticks out in my memory most is the expression of pride and love on Craig's face as his son shared his gratitude with the class.

–Peter Conti

"Who do you know that has regular contact with motivated sellers?"

This question leads you to create a network of people who can refer motivated sellers to you. For example, a divorce attorney has regular contact with many homeowners who want to sell fast. By networking with a divorce attorney, you can help one of his clients out of a painful situation by buying his or her property.

"What can you offer a seller?"

As an investor you offer the seller a variety of things, any one of which might be just what he is looking for. Look back over the seven reasons why motivated sellers sell. In essence, you are working as a problem solver helping the seller of a property. If you are talking with a frustrated landlord, you are offering the seller freedom from the headaches and hassles of managing a rental property. And since the seller still "owns" the property until your tenant-buyer purchases, the seller gets to keep all the tax benefits of owning the property during the term of your agreement.

Or maybe you are talking with someone who is moving. To them, you are offering an instant solution to their problem of having to rent or sell their home. They can stop agonizing over the work it takes to sell or rent the home and focus instead on their upcoming move. We're sure you get the idea now.

The key point to remember is that most sellers are not motivated sellers. The biggest mistake you can make is to try and talk anyone into doing a deal with you. You must sort through sellers until you find the right one. Then, and only then, should you invest your time talking through the details with them. If you do not feel the seller has both the motivation and situation to make working with you a fit—move on immediately.

"Is the house vacant?"

One of the questions you will ask sellers when you're talking to them is: Is the property vacant? (If so, for how long?)

This question allows the seller to share an important clue with you. A house that has ben vacant for any period of time means that the owner is having to:

1. Make payments on the property (mortgage payment, taxes, insurance)
2. Discourage vandals

3. Maintain the property (landscaping and utilities)
4. Try to sell or rent the house

Vacant properties often have a motivated owner. I always get excited when I talk with a student who has a lead on a vacant property. When I see that the property has been vacant for three months or longer, I can picture the stacks of money my student is going to earn.

—Peter Conti

Now you know to always ask if the property is vacant, and if so, for how long. When you do find vacant properties, your chances of putting together money making deals go up tremendously.

How to Turn Your Telephone Into the Biggest Money-Maker of All: Calling Property Owners In the Classified Ads

This concept is by far the fastest and cheapest way to find motivated sellers. It takes a bit of work, but it is a great training ground to learn how to quickly sort through property owners to find motivated sellers.

In this section, you are going to learn how to transform your telephone and local paper into a steady stream of moneymaking deals. These lead sources are readily available to you. They are cheap, fast, and effective. When you apply the strategies and skills you learn in this section on a consistent basis, you will make consistent profits. It is that simple.

The neat thing about using the telephone is that you have the ultimate safety net—hanging up! The seller may try and say something mean to you, but you've got complete control. If someone is not in a good mood when you talk to them, you can politely hang up the phone after wishing them a good day. Besides, talking on the phone gives you a certain anonymity and freedom. Have fun putting this into effect. Think of it as your cash-creating playground.

Many beginning investors go wrong by trying to talk people into doing a deal. That's completely backwards. Rather than chasing down sellers and talking them into doing a deal with you, what you want to do is find people who will ask you to tell them more about your potential solutions. The critical difference is that they are now coming after you, you are not going after them.

How to Find a Motivated Seller in Two Minutes or Less!

As an investor, your most valuable asset is time. You must constantly be protective of your time and only invest it where you will get the greatest return. One of the biggest mistakes new investors make is spending their precious time talking with sellers who just are not motivated or flexible.

But you are going to safely sidestep this pitfall by learning to use the following Quick Check scripts. These Quick Check scripts are designed to help you talk with a property owner, and within two minutes, find out whether or not they are a motivated seller. You will call property owners and take them through the appropriate Quick Check script. If they pass the script, you have a motivated seller. These sellers are worth investing your time to talk with at greater length. If the seller fails at any point in the script, politely end the conversation and move on to your next call.

The "For Rent" Quick Check Script

Right now we are going to walk through the rental property Quick Check script. Advertisers in the "For Rent" section have already demonstrated that they are willing to allow someone to come in and take control of their property with a small amount of money. (After all, that is basically what you do when you rent a property. You go in, give them a month's rent and a month's security deposit, and you have full and complete control of that property through the term of the lease.)

81

"Hi, this is _____. I was calling on your ad... It sounds like I caught you in the middle of something?"

When you first call someone on the phone, their initial thoughts are, "Who is this person and what are they trying to sell me?" But you are going to be different. You are going to be clumsy and vulnerable on the phone. And because you are in a sense, helpless, the person you are talking with will want to reach out and help you.

This specific language is very powerful. Nine times out of 10 when you say to a seller, "It sounds like I caught you in the middle of something," they will say, "no." Better still, they will reach back out to you and ask what they can do to help you. It works. We strongly recommend you not change a word of it.

"Is your property still available?"

Obviously if it isn't, then you move on to your next call.

"Can you tell me about the property?"

You are not concerned about the features of the property at this point, you are just building rapport with the owner. Listen for a short while, then break in and ask the next question. **CAUTION!** Many sellers will go on and on about all the features of their home. This can eat up your precious time. Make sure you avoid this by going to your next question.

"That's great, I'm looking for a long-term lease of at least two years, is that OK?"

If they aren't open to at least two years, how are you going to talk to them about leases of four to eight years? The minimum time for a Purchase Option deal is two years. The only way you will go with a shorter term is if the seller significantly discounts the price of the property.

"Assuming all my rental payments came in to you on time, would you consider selling at the end of two years?"

This is the major qualifying question with a rental property—is the owner willing to sell the property. Notice the nice, gentle progression into discussing you buying their rental property.

"Because I'm an investor who focuses only on nice homes in nice areas, can you tell me, is yours a nice home in a nice area?"

This question is crucial *not* for the information it will help you gather, but rather for the information it will help you *share*. A while back many of our students were running across one objection over and over again when talking with property owners. When the seller found out they were speaking with an investor, they balked.

That's when we developed this single question that cures this objection *before* it ever comes up. Because you are asking the seller if their property is a nice one, they willingly accept the beginning of that question—that you are an investor. When you use this question, 90% of the time, the seller never mentions again that you are an investor.

The key point to remember with this question is *not* to pause after the word, "investor." Read straight through the beginning of the question. The emphasis is placed on whether their home is a nice home in a nice area, not on the fact that you are an investor.

This one question alone is exactly the kind of insider's tip that you need to take your real estate investing to the next level.

"One last question, this sounds like a wonderful property… why would you ever consider selling it?"

This question is key for you to uncover the seller's real motivation. Listen closely to the answer. Does he have a real motivation to sell or is he just curious to hear what you have to offer? You need to guard your time and invest it only with the truly motivated sellers out there whom you can help.

If they have made it through the Quick Check Script this far, chances are you have a motivated seller on your hands. Set up an appointment for him to show you the property. Then you'll want to sit down with him to see if you can put together a winning deal.

The "For Sale" Quick Check Script

On a "For Sale" property, the owner has already indicated a willingness to sell. The big question that you'll need answered, is whether he is going to need money out of this sale to go buy another property immediately. (I.e. Is he flexible on the terms of the sale—can he carry a note for some or all of the equity? Is he open to a lease-option? Etc.)

Let's walk through the "For Sale" Quick Check script line by line.

"Hi, this is _____. I was calling on your ad. Sounds like I caught you in the middle of something?"

84

We've already covered this part and the next two questions as well.

"Is your property still available?"

"Can you tell me about the property?"

Remember that you are not concerned with all the features of the property at this point. You just need to let them talk to you about the house so that you can ask them the next question, which is crucial:

"This sounds like a wonderful property, why would you ever consider selling it?"

This question will let you know if you are really dealing with a motivated seller. Listen to see where the seller's answer fits in with the seven causes of motivated sellers you learned about earlier in this section.

"Because I'm an investor who focuses only on nice homes in nice areas, can you tell me, is yours a nice home in a nice area?"

"Well I don't know if there is a reason for us to be talking or not. As an investor, I have several different methods to buy your home. One method is for me to lease your property for a year or two and then completely cash you out of the home. Is that something we should talk about or probably not?"

This is the core-qualifying question for a person selling their home. In essence, you are asking them if they are flexible on the terms of the sale.

As a real estate investor, you need sellers who are flexible on either the price or the terms. If they are flexible on the price, then they are willing to sell you the property at a significant discount (*at least* 25% below market value.) If they are flexible on the terms, they don't need to be cashed out of all their equity up front, and they are prime candidates for a Purchase Option offer.

Why do you phrase this question as a negative? Why does the script ask, "Is this something we should talk about or *probably not*?" The reason is that we have found that by being a bit negative at this point, your success rate will dramatically increase.

You have set things up where you aren't coming on like gangbusters—you're being a bit reluctant and this spurs them to work to convince you this is something they are interested in. The easiest way I have found to do this is to present your qualifying question in a negative manner. When you say, "For example, one of the things we do is lease your property for a few years and then cash you out at the end of the time period. That probably wouldn't work for you, would it?" they can say one of two things.

They could say, "No, it wouldn't." (Which, by the way, 8 out of 10 people—maybe more—will be telling you.) "That won't work for me. I need the money from this house to go and buy my next house in the other state where we are being moved." Well, if that's the case, you simply wish them luck and move on to your next call.

However, they might also tell you, "Well, you know, we'd be open to talk to you about that." That is where you move on and set up the appointment to meet with them.

(NOTE: When you are using this take away technique, it is critical for your voice tone to go DOWN on the final part of your negative question. For example: "Is that something we should talk about, or (your voice gets deeper) probably not?" Remember, if your voice goes up at the end, you sound too eager. When your voice goes down, you sound like the reluctant buyer you want to be. This one tip alone will make you much better on the phone.)

When you find a seller that passes the Quick Check script you simply set up an appointment to view the property. Then you will sit down and talk through things to see if you can find a win-win agreement. (We'll go into exactly what you will say when you meet with the seller later in this book.)

How to Increase Your Phone Effectiveness by 400% by Letting Your Ads "Age"

Ads that are a few weeks to a few months old are best. The reason these aged ads are best is because time has done a good deal of your sorting for you. If a person has been trying to sell a property for several months with no luck, chances are they will be more motivated than the seller who has just put their home on the market six days earlier. The same thing is true for landlords. There is nothing more unnerving for a landlord than to have a property vacant for two or three weeks.

Aging your ads is simple. Just create a pile from your local paper's classified section. Each day or week put the current ads in the pile and let time do its magic for you. You want to age your rental property ads two to three weeks, and age your properties for sale ads one to three months.

Obviously, many of the people you call from these aged ads will have handled their property some time ago. This is fine. Simply congratulate them and move on to your next call. The best part is that it will take you less than 30 seconds to find this out and then you'll be on to your next call.

The property owners who are still looking for a buyer or a renter will be thrilled that you called. And since these are the types of people you want to talk to, it just makes sense that you would want to call out of an older newspaper. You get a lot more people who will get off the phone quickly with you because they have already taken care of their property. But those people who still have property available are definitely motivated. Our students have found this one simple bit of wisdom to mean up to *400 percent better results*!

Is there some advantage to calling on fresh newspaper classified ads? In our minds, the benefits of doing that do not outweigh the advantages of being able to speed through the newspaper, having the people already pre-sorted by time, so that you are only talking with those people who are highly qualified. Does that make sense? You can always test things out on your own by making 100 calls to current ads and 100 calls to month-old ads. Our experience and the experiences of our students have taught us the wisdom of this little-known technique.

How to Choose Which Ads to Call First

When you are looking through the "For Rent" ads, immediately screen out any that are offered through either property management companies, real estate companies, brokers or sales agents. The reason for this is you want to be able to talk directly to the owner of the property. It is not that you can't put a deal together through these people, it is just easier in the beginning of your investing if you are able to speak directly with the property owner.

Eliminate any ads that don't look like they'll put you directly through to the owner.
The same rule applies to "For Sale" ads. You are looking for ads that put you in direct contact with the owner of a property.

Of course you are also going to look for other signs that the owner is a flexible seller. Here is a list of language used in classified ads that often indicates a motivated seller:

- FSBO ("for sale by owner"—a good sign!)
- OWC ("owner will carry" the mortgage...i.e., seller doesn't need all cash)
- Lease-option (just what you are looking for... one caution is to make sure they don't want a huge option payment.)
- Moving
- Must sell
- Estate sale
- An out of state phone number in the ad

Other Sources of Leads

We've talked about using "For Rent" and "For Sale" ads in your major newspapers. Let's talk about some of your other sources of leads to call.

A common overlooked source of leads is in your small community newspaper. We recommend that you either find a way to purchase it on a regular basis or subscribe to it and have it delivered to you. If you have more than one community paper, even better... get them all!

The next place you may want to look is on the Internet where there are sellers advertising their properties on the World Wide Web. Search for either "For Rent" businesses in your area who are using the Internet to advertise rental properties for owners or look for a "For Sale By Owner" type of company that has ads available. (Simply go to one of the major search engines like "Yahoo" and type in: "for sale by owner".) You can even find the classifieds of many newspapers on the web, which will save you time and money!

You can scan those ads, get the owners' phone numbers, and run them through the scripts you just learned to see if there is a reason you should be talking to them.

"For Sale By Owner" publications are another incredibly good source for deals. Our students have found that many of the people who advertise in "For Sale By Owner" publications have very little or no equity in their property. These sellers are looking for an alternate means of handling their property in lieu of using a real estate agent, because there's not enough money in the property to pay an agent's commission. Or many times, these sellers simply do not want to pay a large real estate commission on the sale of their property. In either case, you'll find great leads from this source.

Finally, look in the newspaper for organizations that offer products or services to people selling their own homes (e.g. offers to advertise FSBO homes in a specific magazine or on the Internet.) Call those organizations and see if there is a way that you can network with them to get a list of their clients or leads. Ask if they will pass on the names and numbers of all their new customers to you for a fee.

You have just learned the basics of how to turn classified ads into an ever-flowing stream of profitable deals. The ultimate key in converting these leads into cash is the consistency with which you go after them. When you make your calls each and every day, you can't help but make lots of money. That's just the way the numbers work out. So start dialing!

The Stairstep Wealth-Building System

The Stairstep Wealth-Building system is the fastest and most powerful way to get motivated sellers to call you—begging you to buy their property.

This simple three-step system gets motivated sellers to raise their hands and tell you they are interested in learning about how you can help them solve their real estate problems. Next, it helps you qualify these leads. And finally it puts you in direct contact with these sellers, talking with them on the phone.

Step One: Getting Motivated Sellers to Raise Their Hands

Step one is for you to get a motivated seller to call you and say, "Yes, I am interested in hearing about what you can offer me."

The sole purpose of the different marketing materials you use in step one is to get a motivated seller to call you. You can place a classified ad like:

**"I buy houses, no equity, no problem.
Call 303-555-1212. 24 hour rec. msg."**

Or you can put out flyers or posters in the areas you want to buy homes. (See the sample flyer on page 94)

The key point with all your marketing materials is that they should focus on the benefits the seller will get if he will only take one simple step—to call the 24 hour recorded message. You want your marketing materials to do one thing, generate a phone call.

When you ask yourself what you can offer a motivated seller, you are taking the first step to position yourself to be the solution that these motivated sellers have been desperately seeking. When you do this, no longer will you have to go out looking for motivated sellers... now they'll come after you!

Would you like to have scores of motivated sellers chasing you to sell you their property at an incredible price with attractive terms? Then make sure you emphasize in all your marketing materials and media the following benefits you offer motivated sellers:

- Debt relief
- Instant solutions—they can stop agonizing over how to unload the property and pass it on to you
- Cash
- Freedom from the headaches and hassles of maintaining their property
- Time—you'll do all the paperwork for them and free them up from having to look after their property
- Money—if you're not a real estate agent they'll save thousands in commissions
- Security—you are an expert in your field—you'll guide them to make an intelligent decision with their property
- Guaranteed written offer—they can count on your word because you'll put everything in writing for them
- You are getting the idea by now.

Stop for a moment and review the marketing materials you

have been using to attract motivated sellers. Do they focus on the needs and desires of the seller? Do they use rich benefit language clearly spelling out what's in it for them if they sell you their property? If not, you need to update and supercharge your materials. When you focus on the seller and what's in it for them, you will double — even triple the results of your efforts. You'll be making more money with much less effort.

Step Two: Set up a voice mailbox with a benefit laden scripted message to compel callers to leave contact information on your voice mail.

Your scripted message will be 60-120 seconds long and will provide, in rich language, the most compelling benefits you have to offer motivated sellers, if only they will leave you their name and phone number.

Some people ask why not just have all your ads and flyers go to your direct line instead of to a voice mailbox?

There are three reasons for having all calls go to a voice mailbox.

First, chances are if you're like most investors, you're not sitting by your phone all day waiting for calls, are you? So when you're out of your office, what does a caller hear on your machine? (If you're like most people you probably say something like: "Hi I'm away from my office or on the other line right now, but leave a message and I'll call you back as soon as possible." BEEP!)

Sell or Lease
Your House Today!!!

Transferred? Bad Tenants? Need Fast Cash?
Behind on Payments? House Vacant? Moving? Double
Payments? Divorce? Estate Sale?

Here Is Your *Quick* and *Easy* Solution:

- *Fast* Closing — **Even Within 48 Hours**
- *Instant* **Debt Relief!**
- *Cash!!!*
- *Freedom* **From Maintainence Hassles!**
- *Guaranteed* **Written offer Within 48 Hours!**

Call 24 Hr. Recorded Message:
303-555-1212

And In 90 seconds You'll Know Exactly How I Can Help You!!!

24 Hr. Recorded Mesage: 303-555-1212
24 Hr. Recorded Mesage: 303-555-1212
24 Hr. Recorded Mesage: 303-555-1212
24 Hr. Recorded Mesage: 303-555-1212
24 Hr. Recorded Mesage: 303-555-1212
24 Hr. Recorded Mesage: 303-555-1212
24 Hr. Recorded Mesage: 303-555-1212
24 Hr. Recorded Mesage: 303-555-1212
24 Hr. Recorded Mesage: 303-555-1212

If you were calling ads out of the paper searching for a fast solution to a painful real estate problem, would you find that an exciting message? Would that cause you to want to leave your name and number? Of course not, it's boring. And being boring is the ultimate sin of marketing.

Instead when they call your voice mailbox, they get 60-90 seconds of your most compelling thoughts on how you can help them solve their real estate situation. This is 10 times more effective in whetting prospective seller's appetites than the traditional message.

The **second** reason to use a voice mailbox rather than a direct line is that it allows you to give your callers an easy, safe way to find out more about what you have to offer them.

The four magic words that can triple — or quadruple — your response rate from your ads are:

24 Hour Recorded Message

These four words work so well because they offer a caller convenience (24 hours a day) and security (a recorded message—not a live salesperson to talk them into something.)

This is called "stepping up" your prospects. They see an ad (or sign, or flyer) and they call to find out more. They hear a powerful scripted message when they call and, in turn, leave their name, number and other information for you to call them back. Now when you do talk with them on the phone, they have already had two previous contacts with you (the ad itself and then the voice mail message.) This makes finding out about their property and situation easy. It's the natural next step.

The **third** reason to use a voice mailbox rather than a direct line is that your voice mailbox can save you hours of time as a screening device. Simply by putting a few qualifying questions or comments into the scripted message, you can screen out the unwanted and unqualified callers, leaving you only the high-grade ore. The very fact that a caller has to take the extra step of calling a voice mailbox, before you call back, is a qualifying step. Ultimately, this step will allow you to talk with a lot fewer curiosity seekers and a lot more people with properties who have the motivation to sell *fast*.

Step Three: Calling Back the Motivated Seller

Step three is for you to consistently check your voice mailbox and call these sellers back. When you talk with them, you are going to use the following Quick Check script:

"Hi, this is _____. I have a message here that you called me about a property you want to sell?"

"It sounds like I caught you in the middle of something?"

"This sounds like a wonderful property, why would you ever consider selling it?"

By this point you will know if you are talking with a motivated seller or not. If they are motivated, set up the appointment and go out and meet with them.

Ultimately the Stairstep Wealth-Building system is a great way to help you leverage your efforts in finding motivated sellers. It will save you time and make your investing yield more results.

How to Select and Develop Your Farm Area for Fun and Profits

A farm area is an area of your city in which you choose to concentrate your investing efforts. Although it can be a time consuming process, this is a powerful way to create long-term investment opportunities for yourself. While you will still be looking for properties in other areas, a portion of your investing efforts will be focused specifically on your farm area. The benefits to you of taking the time to cultivate your farm area are:

- You'll be an expert on property values and market rent in this area—you'll be able to spot good deals and move quickly to close on them.
- You'll know when a seller isn't telling you the truth about a property's price—this will help you avoid costly mistakes.
- You'll thoroughly understand the selling points of an area that you can share with your tenant-buyer to encourage them to move in.
- Over time this is one of the most effective ways to bring deals to you—you'll save time and effort because people will know about you and how you can help them—they will come looking for you to put together deals.
- Because you have carefully chosen your farm area, you can maximize your profits—you will select an area with high rates of appreciation and strong market rents, turning your options into incredible money making tools.

Characteristics of a Good Farm Area

You need to think about the price range of homes in which you want to invest. Obviously since appreciation is one of the ways you make money with Purchase Option Investing, the more expensive the homes, the more money you will probably make on each deal. What you want to do is find the neighborhood with the price range of homes you would like to invest in using Purchase Option techniques. You should focus on homes that are in the middle to upper-middle portion of the spectrum of homes available in your area. These homes offer the best profit opportunity with the least amount of work. The Purchase Option system; however, can be applied to any priced home you want.

Ideally you are going to pick out a neighborhood with a total of 1,500 to 2,000 homes. What? Are we really saying your farm area only needs to be this big? YES! A farm area of this size, when properly worked over time, will provide profitable deals month after month.

Depending on the demographics of the area and how many renters there are, you're going to have a number of rental homes in that area, too. Our goal is for you to end up having between 300-400 homes that you know might be rentals.

Getting to Know Values in Your Farm Area

Once you've picked out this farm area, one of the things you want to do is drive through it regularly so that you can get to know it. Take different routes so that you go through all of the various streets and get to know the neighborhood.

In addition, we want you to go out and take a walk or ride

your bike in this area. You can see things when you're moving at a slower pace that you're not able to see as you're driving through it.

What is it you're looking for? You are looking for any clues that reveal potentially profitable deals. The best clue is a vacant house. When you see one, write down the property address and do some research to find out who owns it and how you can contact them.

Next, be aware of "for rent" signs. Any time you see a "for rent" sign in your farm area, write down the phone number and address of the property. Follow-up with a phone call using the "For Rent" Quick Check script.

You are also on the lookout for any property with "for sale by owner" signs. Jot down the number and call the owner using the "For Sale" Quick Check script.

One way in which you can get to know your farm area and spread your name throughout it is by handing out flyers. Print up a flyer like the sample you saw on page 93 of this book. (Remember, the number is going to lead to your 24-hour recorded message.)

If you meet someone as you are walking through the neighborhood, have a quick conversation with them about the area. Let them know that you buy real estate, and that you even pay a finder's fee for leads that turn into deals. Also make sure that you ask them about market rents and property values in the area. These people are a hidden source of valuable information many investors overlook. You are beginning your education about values in your farm area. Over time, you will become an expert on this location.

"Farming" Your Farm Area

Start developing a list of people who will work for you as property "bird dogs." A bird dog is someone who lets you know about a seller who might be motivated or flexible. If you are able to put a deal together with this seller, you can even pay a referral fee to the person who told you about the property.

You only pay money after you make more money. This source of motivated sellers has an unlimited upside potential and no downside. You only pay for results! The more quality people that you have referring people to you, the better. We suggest you pay between $250 and $1,000 for each successful referral. This might seem high, but you'll be making thousands more on these deals using your powerful Purchase Option techniques, so the money is worth it.

Examples of good contacts who may want extra income and would make excellent "bird dogs" include:

- Postal delivery people in the area (They even know when a house is a rental, when someone is about to move, or if a house is vacant.)
- Newspaper delivery people
- House-sitting companies
- Moving companies

How to Develop
Money-Making Relationships With
Real Estate Agents

Many investors make the costly mistake of considering real estate agents as competitors. They incorrectly see themselves out in the market competing for a limited number of deals—fighting it out with local agents and brokers to make money. This costs investors time, and it costs them thousands of dollars from lost deals.

The truth is that as an investor, one of the most profitable relationships you can ever develop is with a real estate agent. Think about it for a moment. As an investor, your market is motivated sellers who don't need all cash at closing (and who are willing to be flexible on the terms of sale) or who are willing to deeply discount the price of their properties for an immediate sale.

But the majority of sellers you talk with, as you do your lead generation, are *not* motivated sellers. As many as 90% of the sellers you talk to are not motivated enough to be flexible on price and terms like you need them to be. Most investors toss these sellers into the round file, and this mistake costs them dearly.

Instead, refer those sellers you cannot help to your real estate agent ally. He will be able to turn these sellers into a steady stream of commissions as he lists, then sells their homes. Remember that most agents spend tremendous amounts of time and money to find the very people you turn up in such great numbers—homeowners looking to sell for all cash and who have the time to wait for a top dollar offer. If you can help your agent friend get just one more listing a month, you are adding tens of thousands of dollars to his annual income!

So what's your payoff? Actually, you don't just get one payoff, you get five! Here are your five paydays for teaming up with a real estate agent.

Payday Number One: Expired Listings

A listing is an exclusive agreement a seller signs with an agent giving that agent the right to sell their home. The agreement is typically for three to six months. Sometimes an agent is unable to sell the house within that time period.

Have your agent ally search the MLS (Multiple Listing Service—a database of properties for sale that only real estate agents have access to) looking for properties that didn't sell and whose listing has expired. These owners are far more likely to have grown motivated and are ripe for you, the investor, to call and put a deal together on their house.

In many cases the expired listings will not have a phone number for you to contact the owner. That's good! If it were too easy, then another investor would have beat you to the prize. Simply take the information and do your own research. You can use the street address and a reverse directory to look up the phone number. You can often find a copy available for you to use for free at your local library.

Once you find the phone number, give the owners a call and see if they are flexible enough for you to buy their property.

Payday Number Two: Listings Search

Have your agent friend do a search of the MLS for key words that indicate motivated sellers. The agent simply searches the comments field for words like: "lease-option," "flexible terms," "owc," "moving," "transferred," "estate sale," or "contract for deed."

If a listing has these words in it, chances are pretty good that the seller is worth a phone call. Then you contact these owners and see if you can put a deal together.

Payday Number Three: Straight Referrals

Just as you are out there sorting through sellers, so too is your real estate friend. And when he finds an owner he can't help, but who shows signs of being motivated, your agent can refer the seller to you. Better yet, ask your agent friend to pass along the owner's name and phone number and give him a call yourself. This is a great source of deals that no other investor will know about!

Best of all, this third party referral gives a huge boost to your credibility. In essence, the real estate agent is recommending you to the seller. This makes things much easier for you to put a deal together than if you were just coming in cold.

Payday Number Four: Fast and Free Access to Property Information

When you're out there putting together deals, wouldn't it be valuable to be able to call up your real estate contact and ask him for information like sales comparables, market rents, and rates of appreciation?

If you're passing on several good leads a month to your real estate friend, you will be amazed at how fast he will get back to you with information that he simply pulls up from the MLS. After all, if he isn't fast, there are many agents out there who are dying for your leads who will be much faster.

The most important thing to remember when you are putting together this relationship is to always be willing to give value first. Pass leads on to your agent friend for a while *before* you ever call him up asking for a favor. You will be building trust and enhancing your relationship with him.

Over time this relationship will payoff handsomely for you. When you get the relationship going strongly, you've just added a helper who is working with you to make you more money.

One of our students used this real estate networking idea to find a six-year lease-option on a $200,000 property with nothing down! If he can do it, so can you.

By now your mind is turning over all these exciting ideas and techniques for finding and qualifying motivated sellers. But part of you might be a little nervous about what you are supposed to do when you go out to meet with a seller at his property.

In the next section of the book you will learn about the Instant Offer System—a simple 5-step plan for negotiating with sellers. The Instant Offer System is designed so that anyone, whether they are seasoned investors or are looking to buy their first property, can negotiate like a pro. You will develop the confidence that comes from having a proven formula for creating win-win agreements with sellers.

Section Three:

The Instant Offer System

How To Get Sellers To Say "YES!" To Your Creative Offer

When you meet with a motivated seller to negotiate a deal, there are five specific steps you need to take to establish rapport with the seller, draw out his needs, and finally to get him to say "yes" to your creative offer.

Step 1: Asking The Seller to Show You Around the House

Goal: To establish rapport with the seller.

In its simplest form, rapport is a connection of friendship between two or more people. In step one of the Instant Offer System your goal is to become friends with the seller.

When you get to the house and ring the bell, simply hold out your hand and introduce yourself to the seller.

"Hi Mr. Seller, I'm Joe Investor. It's nice to finally meet you in person. Thanks for inviting me over to show me your property."

Notice you use the word "invite." The seller did invite you over, didn't he? By using that specific word, the seller will see you not just as an investor, but more as a guest.

Now ask the seller to show you around the property. As you go around the house, do your best to get the seller talking about himself and establishing a connection with you.

FORM

To make friends with the seller use the powerful and simple formula called: "FORM"

F amily and friends
O ccupation
R ecreation
M essage

"**F**"amily and Friends: Ask the seller about his family. Where is he originally from? Are his kids all grown up? Get him talking about himself and build as many bridges as possible between what you and he have in common.

For example:

Seller: "This is the family room. It has a gas fireplace—"

You: "Are these your kids in this photograph?"

Seller: "Yes. Of course, they're all grown up now."

You: "Do they still live close?"

Seller: "My son Tommy does. He's a teacher at the local high school." (Seller starts to smile and warm up) "My two children both moved away. My daughter moved to Reno two years ago."

You: "I know how that is… My son just went off to college this year. I miss him already. Is that you at the Grand Canyon in this photo?"

"**O**"ccupation: You can also ask the seller about his work. What does he do for a living? How did he get started in that business? It's another level on which to draw the seller out and to make a close connection with him.

"**R**"ecreation: What does the seller like to do for fun? Pay attention to the house as you walk through it. Ask the seller about the photographs and knick knacks you see so carefully displayed. You'll be amazed at how much fun it can be to tap into the seller's interests.

"**M**"essage: We'll cover this one in just a moment.

Your goal again is to make a friend. It is that simple. Of course you are interested in seeing the property, but that is secondary to building rapport with the seller.

WARNING: It should only take you 5-10 minutes to walk through the house and make a friend. If it takes you longer than that, you need to speed things up or you are investing too much of your time on a property you haven't yet locked-up under contract.

Once you have gone through the house and made friends, it's time for the "Message." Here is your message:

"**Thank you for showing me around your house. Where's a good place for us to sit down and talk this through?**"

Let the seller tell you where he feels most comfortable talking. It might be the kitchen table or it might be the den, the key point is to let the seller tell you where it should be. After all, you want the seller to feel at ease.

When you sit down, it is time for you to move to step 2.

Step 2: The Up-Front Agreement

Goal: To create the context for an immediate decision from the seller on your offer.

The up-front agreement is critical for your peace of mind. It guarantees that at the end of your conversation with the seller, you will know if you are moving ahead with the deal or not.

No more "I'll think it over" to drive you crazy. No longer will you be wondering later in the week what the seller will decide. Never again will you be waiting for that phone call that never seems to come from the seller.

The biggest benefit you get from using the up-front agreement is that you will know right away where you stand. You are OK with a yes or a no. What you will no longer accept is a maybe. You need to protect your time. This means only working with sellers who want to work with you.

Here's the exact wording of an up-front agreement:

"There are four things we need to talk through before I can present you with an offer on your house.

"Mr. Seller, if I share an offer with you that just doesn't work for you are you OK with telling me that?

"Great, that's like you giving me an "F." I want you to know that I'm perfectly all right with a "no."

"On the other hand, if what I share with you does work for you, are you OK telling me that?

"Great, that's like you giving me an "A.""

"At the same time, I'm going to be grading you. Obviously as an investor I'm here to meet your needs and to make a profit. Are you OK with that? If you aren't, then this won't work. Are you sure about that? Great!

"I don't know if I can meet your needs and make a profit. If I can't, then I'll have to give this an "F.""

"If we can figure out a way that I can meet your needs and make a profit, then I'll give you an "A.""

"The only way we will take a next step is if we both give this an "A.""

"I promise up-front to let you know at the end of our conversation here that I'm giving you either an "A" or an "F" so that I'm being respectful of your time and mine. I'm going to ask for the same courtesy in return. Is that fair?"

How could any seller say "no" to extending you "the same *courtesy* in return"? Of course they will agree. And in doing so, they have committed to giving you an answer during your meeting. No more "I'll think it over" answers for you to agonize over!

Of course you will personalize the language of the up-front agreement to fit you. What is essential is that you get the seller's commitment to give you a definite answer about whether or not your offer is a fit. This is the best safeguard you have for your time. Let's move on to step 3.

Step 3: Drawing Out
The Seller's Motivation
For Selling.

Goals: (You have four of them)
   1) To uncover what the seller's real needs are
   2) To cure the seller of the "Ostrich Syndrome"
   3) To eliminate the seller's other options
   4) To uncover the seller's timeline for selling

In step three, you are going to find out what it is the seller really wants from you and why it is he wants to have you buy his house.

Uncovering the Seller's Real Needs

Your opening question is:

"So what were you hoping I could do for you here today?"

Listen to what the seller says. Then draw out his motivation for selling. The only way you can do this is to subtly get the seller to volunteer his problems with his house.

Just how do you do this? By carefully using negative questions that turn what you think is a real concern of the seller into naïve sounding good things. You take what you think is a problem for the seller, apply the following formula, and then tell the seller how that is a good thing. You'll be amazed at how fast the seller will correct you and vehemently voice just how big of a problem it really is for him!

111

The Magic Formula for Getting Motivated Sellers to Admit Their Real Problems

"The good thing is that it's not a problem ____(insert problem)___ right?"

Now you need to say this in an innocent and naïve sounding voice and it works wonders. Here are some examples to show you exactly how this simple formula works:

"The good thing is that if you rent the place out, at least you'll enjoy working with your tenants, collecting the rents and all that, right?"

(Typical seller response: "I hate dealing with renters, it's a big hassle." You then say, "Oh, it's a big hassle? I didn't realize that...")

"It's probably not a problem if you don't sell right now. At least you can move into your new house. And if it takes you six or twelve months to sell this place, at least it won't be a problem to cover both payments, right?"

(Typical seller answer: "No we don't want to have to do that, it would be a real financial strain for us to make both payments." You respond, "Oh, it would be a financial strain for you, I can understand that...")

"If you can't sell right away yourself, the good thing is that you can always list the property with a real estate agent and have them sell it for you. I mean at least you know they are going to earn their [X] percent commission by selling the place for you, right?"

(Typical seller response: "We don't want to list it with an agent, that would cost us [Y] dollars in commissions." You respond, "Oh, yeah I can see how that's a lot of money to pay them out of your equity...")

See how easy it is. In essence you are identifying the negative realities the seller faces. However, you are phrasing it to them in such a gentle way that they will restate it in a stronger form themselves.

Now you can accomplish your second goal—to cure the seller of the "Ostrich Syndrome." The "Ostrich Syndrome" is what happens when the seller is faced with a tough situation. It is commonly referred to as *denial.*

It's a fact of human nature that when we are faced with tough circumstances many of us don't like to look a person straight in the eye. Your job in step three is to help the seller face the reality of the situation. And you have to do it in such a way as to let him voice the bad stuff himself. (Otherwise he will resist it.)

Your third goal is to eliminate the seller's other options. You want the seller to tell you that you are the best option. How do you do this? You eliminate the three major alternatives the seller has:

1) Listing the property with an agent
2) Renting the place out
3) Continuing to try and sell the place himself

Use the magic formula that you have just learned. For example, to eliminate the possibility of listing the property with a real estate agent:

"Why don't you just find an agent to list the property for

113

you? I mean it may take them a few months to sell the place, but I'm sure you'll find a good one who will really earn the commission, right?"

Let the seller convince you why he wants to sell it to you. Here's another example:

"I don't understand why you just don't rent the place. I mean you'll cover your payment and the good thing is that dealing with renters is easy enough, right?"

Is There a Ticking Bomb?

Once you draw out the seller's motivation find out one last piece of information: What is the seller's timeline for selling?

Ask the seller this question:

"Mr. Seller, ideally when would you like your property handled? Do you want it to happen in six to twelve months? Or longer? Ideally when would you like to have this taken care of?"

When you know this critical item, you are in a strong negotiating position to meet the seller's real needs. Notice that you ask him if he wants the property handled in six to twelve months or longer. Most sellers will immediately come back and tell you that they want the property handled much sooner. (The most common answer our students hear is "this month.")

If the seller tells you that he has no real timeline, that he will just wait until the property sells, this is usually a sign that you are *not* dealing with a motivated seller. Make sure you protect your time by being willing to walk away if it becomes clear that it just isn't a fit to work together.

Step 4: Getting Clear on The Financial Details Of the Property

Goal: To draw out the important financial facts.
- **Asking price**
- **Loan balance**
- **Monthly payments**
- **Bottom line price**

In step four, you are going to talk about the financial details of the property. You will then use these financial variables to create your solution to the seller's needs. At this point, you are just gathering information from the seller.

"Mr. Seller, what were you asking for the property?

"And what do you owe against the place?

"And the monthly payment is...? Does that include the taxes and insurance?

"Tell me, what did you really expect to get for the property?"

All of these questions are straightforward. Take a close look at the last question though. It's almost like you are saying to the seller, "Come on, we both know that you're not expecting anyone to give you full price. You'll take a lot less than that, won't you?"

Of course you can't say it that way, so you put it into your facial expression and your tone of voice, "Mr. Seller, what did you *really* expect to get for the house?" Nine times out of ten the price will drop dramatically.

Step 5: The "What If" Game

Goal: To get the seller to agree to the major terms of a deal BEFORE you ever make a formal offer.

Here's your chance to negotiate all the major terms of a deal with the seller before you ever break out an agreement form and write them up an offer. You do this by using the two most powerful words in negotiating: **"What if..."**

Before you get into the "what if's", would you like to know how you can totally reframe the negotiation so what the seller originally thought was a fair deal for them seems out of line? In all likelihood, what did the seller originally want? All cash and full price.

Ask the seller these two specific questions and you'll be floored at how easy it is to completely shift his position to being much more open to working with you:

"Mr. Seller, if I were able to hand you a cashiers check for your full asking price right now, you'd probably take it, wouldn't you? (Seller says "yes")

"Obviously as an investor I can't do that, it's got to work for me too. What if I were to..."

116

This is the time for you to think through what you could possibly offer the seller that would meet his needs and create a large profit for yourself.

For example, if you are going after a lease purchase deal, the following language is incredibly effective.

You: "What if I were to come in and guarantee to make your monthly payments over some period of time, of [X] dollars, that would cover all your costs with the property? And if I were to agree to take care of all the day-to-day maintenance, then at some point during this period, I were to completely cash you out of the property, is that something we should talk about, or probably not?"

Seller: "What price would you be paying and how long a period of time before you cashed me out?"

You: "Well, the price depends on the length of time we decide on. If you want to go with a longer term of 6 to 8 years, then I can probably give you close to your full asking price. I may even be able to give you full price. If you want to go less time than that, then we are going to need to talk about the price. It really is up to you. Would you want to go 6 or 8 years? Or longer? What's the longest period of time that you would feel comfortable with, knowing that it has to work for me too?"

Seller: "Five years is probably the longest I would want to go."

You: (hiding your excitement) "Five years? I don't know if I could do that (being a reluctant buyer). But if I could do that..."

You keep negotiating through the major terms of the deal before you ever make your offer. The best part about this is that if the seller ever says, "no" to one of your "what if" scenarios, he isn't saying, "no" to your offer, merely to one of your trial balloons. If he says, "no", then ask him, "what if …?"(Make another offer.)

Once you come to an agreement to the major terms of the deal, then and only then, bring out the agreement and write it up. You sign it. Then have the seller sign. Next, have the document notarized, if possible. It is that easy when you follow the step-by-step plan of the Instant Offer System.

What Should You Offer The Seller?

There are three major numbers you need to negotiate with the seller. They are:

- Price
- Term
- Rent

So just how much are you willing to pay for the property? In most cases you are going to negotiate the seller down from the asking price. Still, depending on the market you are in, many times price is not the critical factor for you, the investor. The length of time you control the property (the term) can be more important.

If you are in a market that is appreciating faster than 7%, you would probably do better to be more flexible on the price you are offering in exchange for a longer term. In a fast moving market, you will be able to capture between 4-6% of the appreciated value of the property each year you control it. On a typical $200,000 house in an average market, you'd make about $10,000 a year, each year you are in the deal. This amount is just from the appreciation of the property and doesn't include other variables such as, cash flow or option payment.

Of course if you are investing in a slower market, then you will have to negotiate the price down. The best part is that the better you get at negotiating, the more money you will make on each deal.

The term of the agreement is critical to you for two reasons. First, the longer you control the property, the more potential profits you have in the deal. As both the property value and market rent increase, your fixed rent and price become more and more valuable.

Second, the longer you control the property, the lower your risk. You have more time to let the property both increase in value (appreciate) and increase in rental value. The longer your term, the longer you get to enjoy an ever increasingly larger monthly cash flow. Consequently, the longer the term, the more chance you have of selling the property at a good time in the market. Therefore, you have less risk and make more money.

As an investor, you never want to walk into a deal that has a negative cash flow. There are techniques to handle negative cash flow and to get other people to cover it for you. However, when you are starting out, it's never a good idea to move forward in a deal with negative cash flow.

So when you are negotiating with the seller of a property, you are never going to agree to pay higher than market rent for the property. In fact, in most cases you are going to negotiate to pay less than market rent. How? Simply let the seller know that as an investor, you cannot move ahead on a property with a negative cash flow. Since you are going to be the one responsible for the day-to-day maintenance and the cost of finding the right tenant-buyer for the property, the most you can pay without going negative on the property is 85-90% of the market rent. Of course, if you need to, you can let the seller negotiate up a bit higher, but then you need to ask for something back in return, such as a longer term or a lower option price.

[**Editor's Note**: For more information about writing up agreements and protecting yourself in the process, see the Protégé Program in the Success Library, located in Appendix B.]

Here's one final story Peter wanted to share with you about how you can find an ally to help put your deal together. This ally came from an unexpected source.

Patty and Donald had a nice three-bedroom rental home. Patty had explained on the phone that she was tired of dealing with the maintenance hassles and also didn't like the negative cash flow of $75.00 each month.

John and I arrived at about 11:00 in the morning on the last day of the Challenge. We were meeting with Patty, who worked for the airlines, and Donald, a high school counselor, in their nice looking suburban home. After sitting down and building some rapport, we began to learn more about the situation.

Patty was pretty much in charge of dealing with the property. She was responsible for calling the plumber and maintenance man every time something needed fixing. She felt like an awful lot of her free time was spent dealing with various problems regarding the property. Patty wanted the property to look nice when she stopped by to look at it, and the tenants didn't ever seem to keep the property the way she wanted them to.

John explained how we might be willing to use one of the Purchase Option techniques to help out. Patty liked the idea of receiving guaranteed rents from us. Her ears really perked up when John mentioned that we might even be able to handle the maintenance on the property. (We, of course, would get our tenant-buyer to take care of the maintenance.)

While Patty had us convinced that she was ready for us to come up with a solution for her property, Donald was a different story. He sat on a stool with his arms folded, almost daring us to try and convince him. I knew that Patty might become our "helper." I quickly summed up the situation by saying, "Well I know that Patty will like what we have to offer but I don't think Donald will." Donald had told us up to this point that he was basically happy with the way things were going, and he really wasn't interested in making any changes.

"I really don't think we'll be able to help you." I continued. "I just can't see where Donald feels that there is enough benefit in this for him." I was taking the extreme negative approach. You see, most investors will go in and try to "talk" someone into their deal. I wanted to see if I could get Patty to talk Donald into this deal. "Donald, tell me, where are you on a scale of one to ten? With one indicating that you can't wait for me to leave, and ten means that you want to do this and just need me to fill out the paperwork?"

Donald then went into a big explanation of why the property was fine just the way it was and that the only downside was listening to so much "whining from Patty", to use his words. He didn't mention a specific number, but my guess was that he was about a five on the scale, which means no deal.

What happened next surprised John, but not me. Donald and Patty started arguing over whether or not this was a good deal for them. Patty of course wanted it because she was the one who was responsible for dealing with the property. Donald had some good points but was losing the battle against his wife's arguments toward signing the deal with us. Donald still hadn't given me a number from one to ten. John and I just sat there listening and letting the drama play out.

Five minutes later, Donald, transformed by this little exchange with his wife, indicated that he was very close to a ten on the scale and wanted us to write up the deal. What a change! Donald looked so much better smiling than he did before when he was scowling. John went out to get the offer form while I made some more small talk. Ten minutes later we were heading out the door with a signed deal in hand.

It felt especially good to shake Donald's hand knowing that we were able to come up with a win/win deal for everyone.

We ended up with a five-year lease-option to buy at the current market value. Patty and Donald agreed to still cover the $75.00 a month negative cash flow for the next five years. That house is now worth $20,000 more than our option price and we still have over three years left on our option.

—Peter Conti

Section Four:

How to Find Hungry Tenant-Buyers

It's been three weeks and your rental property has been sitting empty — the mortgage payment is due in seven days. Or you got a great buy on a property that you then fixed up. Only now you haven't been able to sell the house and you've already had to make two payments.

Have you ever been faced with either of these scenarios? Let's face it, sometimes finding a good tenant takes hard work. Sometimes finding a qualified buyer just doesn't seem possible.

You must have asked yourself, *"Is there a better way to enjoy all the benefits of great tenants and qualified buyers without the bad stuff?"* The answer is a resounding "YES!" You're now going to learn a step-by-step system to do it.

The Problem and the Solution

Renters can be great. They provide great opportunities, such as monthly cash flow and paying down your loans. However, the best reward of all is that while they do this, you are earning thousands of dollars as your property appreciates in value!

So if renters are so great, how come most people don't want to become landlords? The answer is simple. Great tenants are wonderful, but bad tenants can make your life a mess!

Some renters may not pay the rent, or trash your property, or call you at 3:00 a.m. to come over and plunge their toilet!

Still, there is a way that you can enjoy all the benefits of renting (like cash flow, equity build-up, and property appreciation) without having to deal with the traditional hassles of renters. Before we share with you exactly how you can do this, you need to realize that it gets even better!

You also get all the advantages of a traditional buyer for the property! That's right, not only do you get the benefits of renting, but you also get the huge payoff of someone *buying* your property. That means they'll care for it, and they'll pay you *top dollar* for it. How?

Meet the tenant-buyer. A tenant-buyer is completely different from the traditional renter and the traditional buyer. You must understand the differences to find them.

Traditional renters are looking only for a place to live for the moment. They are not attached to a particular property and have little vested interest in seeing that a property stays nice. After all, if the property goes downhill they can simply pack up and move on.

Tenant-buyers on the other hand, are desperately seeking a place of their own. They want to join thousands of other Americans in one of the strongest callings in our culture: home ownership. But for one reason or another they lack the resources to go out and get a home the traditional way.

Buying a home the traditional way means putting a chunk of cash down, getting a loan for the balance, and paying off the balance over 30 years. Did you know that many Americans can't qualify to buy a home the traditional way?

They lack one (or all) of the three requirements of traditional buying:

1) A large down payment
2) Good credit
3) Steady monthly income (Read "employee" – banks often have more stringent requirements for self-employed people.)

The traditional way of buying a home fails to serve many people who desperately want to own a home of their own. But you can help correct this tragedy by helping these masses own homes. You're going to be helping those people who have been forced into renting, and who really want to escape into owning.

Why Wouldn't a Tenant-Buyer Just Buy a Home Now?

The reasons that a tenant-buyer needs you are almost as varied as the number of tenant-buyers out there. Some of the reasons we see are glitches on a tenant-buyer's credit report. For example, if a tenant-buyer had a bankruptcy five years ago, he probably couldn't qualify for a mortgage for another two years because, in most cases, a bankruptcy stays on a credit report for seven years.

In this case, you'll be able to put this tenant-buyer into one of your investment properties, collecting above average rents and an option payment, while your tenant-buyer waits for time to improve his credit. Once two years go by, your tenant-buyer simply goes out and gets a new loan, cashing you out of the property.

Why Self-Employed People Make Great Tenant-Buyers

Getting a loan when you are self-employed has never been easy. Many self-employed people take advantage of small business deductions, making it hard for them to qualify for a loan.

The truth is that most self-employed people have more control over their future earnings than someone who works for a big company. The nice thing about self-employed tenant-buyers is they normally don't have any problem moving funds around to come up with the option payment.

Why Would You Ever Want a Security Deposit When You Can Get an Option Payment?

"Renters" pay a security deposit that they expect to get back when they move out. Tenant-buyers, on the other hand, will pay you a lot more money in the form of a non-refundable option payment. This is like a down payment, it's money that shows your tenant-buyer is serious and will take care of the property. You are going to collect three to five percent of the house's value as an up-front option payment from your tenant-buyer.

The big difference between a security deposit and an option payment is that if your tenant-buyer decides not to buy the house, then you get to keep the option payment. This reason alone is enough to abandon the "old school" techniques and move on to easier and bigger profits through Purchase Option investing.

Why "Rent to Own" Makes Sense For Your Tenant-buyer

Mary and Bill were expecting their first child in six months. They had wanted to have their own home for years. However, due to a medical problem a few years back, Bill's credit wasn't perfect. Mary found an ad that one of our students, Dan, had placed in the paper. It said:

RENT TO OWN 3 bedroom, 2 bath,
fenced back yard. Close to schools and
shopping. $975/Month Call Dan 555-1234

"Perhaps this is our chance to get into a home before the baby comes," Mary mentioned to Bill that evening. They called Dan and set up an appointment to see the property the next day.

The home was located in a nice suburban neighborhood. Mary and Bill were thrilled when Dan took their check for $3,500 as an option payment and let them know they could move in at the end of the month.

Dan was happy too. He was going to be collecting $975 a month in an area where the average rent was only $900 a month. In addition, he had a tenant-buyer who was willing to pay $115,000 for the house. This was almost $15,000 more than the option price Dan had negotiated with his motivated seller. The reason Bill and Mary were willing to agree to this deal was because with appreciation, the home should be worth even more than their $115,000 price when they actually buy it.

In addition, Mary gets to have her nursery all set up in time for their first child. Bill is excited because he can make improvements to the home, which will increase its value, knowing that very soon the home will be his.

You are helping your tenant-buyers build equity in their home *before* they ever technically purchase it.

Three Ways Your Tenant-Buyer Can Build Equity Before They Ever "OWN" the Property

First, you will often credit a percentage of your tenant-buyer's monthly rent toward the purchase price of the home. This huge benefit helps them build up more equity faster than if they had a traditional mortgage. On a traditional loan, each month they made their payment, only a small percentage of the payment goes to pay down the loan balance. In the first five years, it's only about one percent! Because you are crediting your tenant-buyers up to 20-40 percent of the rent toward the purchase of the home, you are helping them build equity up to **forty times faster** than a traditional home loan!

Second, you are letting your tenant-buyer get a healthy portion of the house's future appreciation. Since you will typically capture 75 percent of the home's appreciation, your tenant-buyer will get the other 25 percent increase in value. A few years later when they purchase, the appreciation of the property itself will have created a healthy chunk of equity for them.

Third, your tenant-buyer can do physical improvements to the property to create "sweat equity" in the home. Some high leverage improvements, such as landscaping, adding on a room, or finishing a basement, add thousands of dollars to the value of a home.

Again, what you are really doing is helping your tenant-buyers own a home in a way that they probably could not have done without you. You are providing them with such value that they are willing pay you higher than market rents, agree to do the minor maintenance on a property, and give you a *non-refundable* option payment up front.

Now it's time to get to the specific game plan for you to go out and FIND your hungry tenant-buyer.

The Overview:
The 12 Steps You Need to Take to Find Your Hungry Tenant-Buyer — Fast!

1) Set up a voice mailbox with a benefit-laden, scripted message to compel callers to leave contact information.
2) Spread the word about the property.
3) Know your market.
4) Work through the numbers on the home to know your tenant-buyer's options.
5) Retrieve your voice mail messages daily and call people back to further qualify them.
6) Set up showings for the property.
7) Make sure the house shows well by doing or contracting out critical cleaning work.
8) Get to the property before each showing to do any last minute preparations.
9) After showing the property to prospective tenant-buyers, collect completed applications right on the spot.
10) Screen applicants and select your tenant-buyer.
11) Call and share the good news with the lucky tenant-buyer.
12) Meet with the tenant-buyer to fill out the final paperwork and collect your money.

Each of these twelve steps takes place in one of three simple phases of your efforts.

Phase One is about spreading the word.

You have a property available that will make some lucky tenant-buyer jubilant. It's your duty to let as many potential tenant-buyers as possible know about this opportunity. (It's also important to do this in the most cost-effective manner — it's your money, after all!)

You can spread the word about the property by placing classified ads, using flyers and posters, telling real estate agents and brokers in the area, setting up an enticing voice mail message, etc... I think you get the idea.

Phase Two is about prepping the property and showing it to your prospective tenant-buyers.

The key here is to protect your time by doing only critical cleaning, and by setting up group showings, if possible. You will soon learn more about these two key points, which will save you hours of frustration!

Phase Three is about closing the sale with your tenant-buyer and completing the paperwork.

The best part about phase three is that it is so much easier than you might imagine.

Are you ready to get into the nitty-gritty detail of it all? Great, let's go!

Step One: Set up a voice mailbox with a benefit-laden scripted message to compel callers to leave contact information so you can call them back.

Your scripted 60-120 second message should detail in rich language, the most compelling benefits you have to offer. You are applying the same powerful stair-step wealth-building technique you learned about earlier to help find tenant-buyers now.

Voice Mailbox vs. Answering Machine

While you can use an answering machine set up on an independent line, we recommend a rented voice mailbox for three specific reasons:

1) You'll save money.

In order to have an answering machine with the specialized message on it set up to take all your calls 24 hours a day, you would need to pay for a separate phone line in your office or home. This would cost close to twice as much as a rented voice mailbox.

2) You'll save hours of frustration and hundreds of wasted dollars.

Sadly, answering machines tend to act up when used frequently. Voice mailboxes are much less trouble and have greater outgoing message clarity.

3) You'll have your voice mail working for you 24 hours a day, 7 days a week.

Your voice mailbox has its own independent number so you can use it freely in your marketing efforts. In addition, this mailbox will be available even when you are not. And since you will have a specialized voice mailbox just to attract and screen tenant-buyers, the message will be tailored to that purpose, which means more profits for you.

You'll probably only need to set up your voice mailbox once because you will keep it constantly in use creating a ready reserve of tenant-buyers for you. Thus, it's worth the 15 minutes it will take you to look up "voice mail" in your local yellow pages and gather 3-5 numbers to call and compare service and prices. You'll want a service that offers the following features:

1) Unlimited messages
2) An outgoing message time of at least two minutes
3) The ability to answer multiple calls at the same time
4) Competitive rates

[**Editor's Note:** The American Real Estate Investor's Association offers its members a great deal on an investor voice mail service. Go to www.americanreia.com, or see Appendix A for details.]

Your Voice Mail Script
Create a script for your outgoing voice mail message to potential tenant-buyers.

Four key points to remember with respect to your voice mail script:

1) Follow the "Rule of Five"
This means that you must have at least five powerful benefits on your message that your caller will get only if he takes one simple, easy step... leave a message with his contact information for you.

2) Read your script with a smiling, warm, friendly voice

3) Follow up as quickly as possible on your good leads

The best time to call someone back is the same day that they left the message. The longer you take to call them back, the lower your success rate will be.

4) Think twice before you ever mention price on your voice mail script

Let's face it, as soon as you mention any specific numbers with respect to price, your caller is going to immediately make a decision about the property… without ever learning more about it. You can use price on your message as a qualifier to screen out poor leads and save yourself time. But we recommend you only do this if you have so many voice mail responses that a return phone call from you is too time intensive.

Once you have the voice mail set up, you can move on to step two.

<u>Step Two:</u> Spread the word about the property.

Call your local newspaper and place your classified ad(s); place a sign in front of the house; put signs up all around the neighborhood; place flyers in high traffic neighborhood locations; talk with high leverage professionals about the property.

You can use classified ads, flyers, signs, referrals, or any number of methods. Each of which will direct prospects to your voice mailbox where they will receive a groomed sales message from you. This way, when you call them back to follow-up, they will be eager to talk to you since they have already received a tasty sample of the benefits you have to offer them from your voice mail message.

Step Two: Spread the word about the property. This is where you get as many tenant-buyers as possible to raise their hands and tell you they are interested in renting to own their next home. The more hands you raise, the more competition you will create for your property. The more competition, the higher the price you can get, the more rent you can charge, and the faster you'll close the deal. (You'll learn more about creating competition for your properties through group showings in step six.)

When you use your voice mail number in your marketing materials, always follow it with "24 hour recorded message." Here's why this is so effective:

- People feel safer calling a recording — they know they won't get "sold" something they don't really want.
- Your tenant-buyers know they can call 24 hours a day, not just during business hours. You will get more calls from people who see your ad/flyer/etc. after hours.

We recommend that you don't change the final four words in your ad. They work. They have been tested and proven to work in the only test that counts — real life. You can abbreviate them to save money. (E.g. 24hr. rec. msg.)

The Four Fastest Ways to
Advertise Your Properties

Let's briefly walk through how to use four of the biggest guns at your disposal to spread the word:

1) Classified Ads:

Without question, one of the most cost effective places you can advertise your properties is the classified section of appropriate publications. Make sure your classified ads focus on the benefits a tenant-buyer receives if they take your property. We have found these ads to work best when they are short and lead directly into a voice mail message.

The sole purpose for a classified ad is to generate a phone call. That's it. It isn't to sell a house or rent an apartment. It can't do that. But it can put you in touch with people who will become your tenant-buyer.

Here is a sample classified ad you can use:

RENT TO OWN 3Br, 2 Ba,
beautiful view, 30% rent credit,
call 303-555-1234. 24 hr. rec. msg."

2) Signs in Front of the House and Around the Neighborhood:

You should have signs made and ready to put up in the front yards and in the windows of your properties. This will allow you to capture the attention of traffic passing through the area. Have the phone number on each sign lead to your voice mail message for that property. You can even

136

add a box of flyers under the sign spelling out the biggest benefits the property offers.

You can also place your signs on telephone poles near the house. Make sure to put the property address on the sign and post it high enough so some rambunctious youth won't prematurely pull it down.

Dollar for dollar, signs are the most effective way to find your tenant-buyer. You can even buy poster board and make your own signs. It doesn't matter as long as you have made it easy for people in the area to know about your property. Ideally you should put at least 15-30 signs around the area, especially on high traffic streets.

3) Neighborhood Flyers:

Where do people who are likely to desire and are able to afford your property, go? Put your flyers in those areas. Examples of good places to consider: grocery stores, major employers in the area, malls, on doors within one mile of the home, and other nearby locations where lots of people go.

4) Referrals from Key People in the Area:

Who in your area has contact with people that might want to rent or buy your property? Maybe local real estate agents, or local bankers, or hairdressers… you get the idea. Are there any major employers in the area? Talk with their personnel department and let them know that you can help them with new transfers. Enroll these people into your network by offering them something in return for their help. Either pay them a referral fee or treat them to a nice dinner.

137

Step Three: Conduct a market survey.

It's imperative to know the property's current market value so you can develop an appropriate rent and selling price.

I remember one student who was having trouble finding a tenant for a property she had under contract. She had the property locked up as a lease purchase on a four-year term for monthly payments of $1005. She was marketing the property as a rent-to-own home with rent payments of $1195.

The problem was that she was one month into her search and she still hadn't found a tenant-buyer. Several people came through the house, but none were interested. She was ready to hand the property back over to the seller, but I asked her to go back and do a rent survey of the area. She discovered that the market rent for this type of house in this area was $1100.

I then advised her to drop the rent to $995 and call back the people who had already seen the house to tell them she would drop the rent — $200 below market rent — but only if they agreed to take the home by Saturday. (Of course the rent increased in the second year to $1075.) By reducing the rent, my student was able to save a deal that she was ready to drop. She even made a large profit, by using the up-front option payment from her tenant-buyer, to cover the property's small negative cash flow.

She was able to complete this deal because she clearly understood the tremendous value she had to offer, with respect to the rent that she was asking. When she dropped the rent so low, she was able to create a sense of urgency, which filled the property right away.

—Peter Conti

How to Conduct Your Rent Survey

There are people living in the neighborhood where your property is located that will tell you exactly how much they are currently paying in rent. This will give you a real life "range" of rents that the market is willing to pay for your property.

To find out how much you'll be able to get, simply go for a walk through the neighborhood where your property is located. By knocking on a few doors, you'll soon find either an owner or most likely a tenant, who will share what he knows about rent levels in the area.

Your conversation with this person is designed to uncover exactly what people are now paying and might be willing to pay for rents in the area. This is very valuable information. You just knock on the door and say:

"Hi, I'm an investor in the area, and I'm looking to rent a house nearby. I was wondering if you might be able to share with me how much folks in this neighborhood are paying in rent."

You, of course, are going to be offering your property as a "rent to own" property so you should be able to command rent that is in the top end of the range. It is assumed that your property is in good shape and shows well.

How to Determine the
Current Value of Your Property

Figuring out just what your property is worth can be done in one of two ways:

139

The *hard* way... or
The *easy* way

You can come up with values the hard way by doing the research yourself. You'll need to subscribe or have access to an on-line database of home sale prices in the area. The problem with this approach is that it takes a while to learn how to use a new system. Consequently, while you're learning the system, you could be out getting another deal or two.

Or, you can take the easy route by befriending a local real estate agent. They invest a lot of time and money into knowing the selling prices of properties in their markets. You can take advantage of this information by connecting with an agent who is willing to share some of their knowledge with you.

Step Four: Work through the numbers on the home to know what you want from your tenant-buyer.

You need to know what questions to ask of your prospective tenant-buyer. You will then be much more effective when you walk them through the property or even when you qualify them on the phone.

What amount will you require as an option payment? What's the rent? Is there any "discount" for early payment? What is the sale price? What's your negotiating range? What kind of terms are you prepared to offer?

**How to Know What to Ask For
From Your Tenant-Buyer**

Knowing exactly how much money to ask for from your tenant-buyer is an important issue. Ask for too little, and you'll be missing out on thousands in profits that you could have easily had. Ask for too much, and you'll soon be frustrated because every tenant-buyer will be coming up with one reason or another that they don't want the house.

The basic concept you will use to guide your investing is this—always leave some of the money on the table to share with the other party. You'll find that your deals go together easier and faster than if you try to keep all the money for yourself.

For example, one of our students, Eddie, found a house that he could lease for $995 a month. He negotiated an option to buy for $125,000 at any time during the next 5 years. This price was $10,000 below the current value of the property. He was able to offer this price by explaining to the seller that if they listed the house, they would only be getting $125,000 after paying a real estate agent's commission.

Eddie knew that he would be making about $30,000 within the next five years when his tenant-buyer got a new loan and cashed him out of the house. He also wanted a big monthly cash flow. The problem was that the rent surveys indicated that market rents in the area were only $900 to $950 for a normal rental and $995 for a rent to own home. (Remember, Eddie agreed to pay his seller $995 a month)

Eddie insisted on asking $1200 a month in rent even though that amount was $200 a month more that the rent surveys indicated he should charge. Eddie was getting greedy, and he was about to find out what happens to greedy investors. He invested at least five hours sprucing up the house and showing it several times. In the end, he had to give the property back to the seller because he was unable to get a tenant-buyer for the property.

Eddie lost out on his long-term profit of $30,000 just

because he was trying to make too much out of the deal. If he had only lowered his monthly rent to $995 for the first year, with annual increases of $50 a month, he would have kept the deal, along with most of his $30,000 profit.

Splitting Up the Pie:
How to Know How Much
Profit to Keep for Yourself

One of the biggest benefits that you have to offer your tenant-buyer is that they'll be able to buy the house at a price that is lower than what the home is expected to be worth in the future. Any future value is going to be a "projected" number. So, by looking at what has been going on with the real estate market in your area, you'll be able to make a good estimate of just how much the values are expected to go up over the next few years.

What you're going to want to do is keep a large portion of the increase in value for yourself, while giving your tenant-buyer enough of a deal so that they will move quickly to snatch it up. For example, if the homes in your area were expected to increase in value by 8 percent a year, the price that you might offer your tenant-buyer would look like this: See chart 5 on page 143. If you were making an extra $100 a month in cash flow, you would add another $3,600 to your three-year profit of $31,525 to come up with $35,125 in total profits.

If the appreciation is higher in your area, simply adjust your numbers up. If appreciation is not quite so strong, you'll adjust the numbers down. What you'll always want to do is share a small portion of the expected future appreciation with your tenant-buyer so that they realize they've gotten an incredibly good deal.

Of course before you get to go spend this money, you need to finish steps five through twelve and find your tenant-buyer.

Step Five: Retrieve your voice mail daily and call potential tenant-buyers back to further qualify them.

It's important to get back to the people who have left a message as soon as possible, even if you are only able to leave a message in return. This lets them know that you received their message and allows you to tell them what their next step is—to see the property.

Step Six: Set up showings for the property. Whenever you can, you want to set up group showings for your properties — not private showings.

Why? Two reasons:

• It will save you time. You can drive over to the property once, not three or more times. Also, you only need to prep the property once, not three or more times.

• You are creating competition for the property. When your guests look around the property and see two or three other people who want to rent to own the property, the competition heats up. People become much more emotionally eager to commit to your property when others are present and enthusiastic.

Chart 5

When	Investor's Option price	The Home value goes up at 8% Appreciation	Tenant-buyer gets to buy home for 5% appreciation	Your long Term Profits	Tenant-buyer's equity from appreciation
Now	$200,000	$200,000	$200,000	N/A	N/A
End of Year 1	$200,000	$216,000	$210,000	$10,000	$6,000
End of Year 2	$200,000	$233,280	$220,500	$20,500	$12,780
End of Year3	$200,000	$251,942	$231,525	$31,525	$20,417

This chart shows the thinking process you'll go through when you determine your tenant-buyer's price. In this example, the house is valued at $200,000 and the tenant-buyer is renting to own over a three-year term.

144

To set up your group showing, simply call back each of your prospective tenant-buyers and set up a *definite* appointment to show them the property. Notice you set up a "definite appointment" not a "showing." This will dramatically increase the percentage of people who show up. Coincidentally, all of your "appointments" will be for the exact same time!

Step Seven: Make sure the house shows well by doing or contracting out high-leverage cleaning work.

You'll want your tenant-buyers to start thinking; "I could see myself living here." The best way to achieve this is to create an atmosphere that is neutral and clean enough that your tenant-buyers can imagine their things in the home.

Just take a little bit of time prepping the property so that you can make sure your tenant-buyer's first impression is a good one. You'll be able to get more rent for the place or sell at a higher price.

Big, Clean, Neat...
The Three Keys for You to
Get Top Dollar in Rent and Price

Everyone desires to have things in their life arranged in neat, orderly compartments. Take a look around at the next successful business franchise that you enter. I think you'll find that the floors and walls are clean and spotless. The products for sale will be arranged into neat, orderly stacks on the shelves.

We all crave order in our lives. It is appealing and compelling to see neat, tidy organized rooms.

You'll want to make the home look as big as possible. In addition, you'll want to clear away anything that might distract your tenant-buyer and get them thinking about something other than, "When can I move in here?" As for cleanliness, is there anything that turns off a prospective tenant-buyer more than someone else's dirt and grunge?

Step Eight: Get to the property before each showing and do a last minute preparation of the house.

To prepare the property, get there at least 15 minutes early, to do any last minute touches. One idea is to put a few drops of vanilla into the oven and let it bake for 15 minutes or so. The whole house will smell of fresh cookies — a great association for your prospective tenant-buyer to make.

Make sure you turn on all the lights and open up all the windows. The home will seem bigger and more open. Are there any footprints in the entryway? Is the kitchen counter free of dust? By having a few minutes at the property before your prospective tenant-buyers arrive, you can take care of any unforeseen problems that inevitably will come up.

Step Nine: Show the property to prospective tenant-buyers and collect completed applications for the property right on the spot.

I have found that the easier the application is to fill out, the more I am able to collect, giving me a better choice of tenant-buyers for the property. The perfect time to collect the completed application is right after they have seen the house and are still emotionally involved with it.

—DAVID FINKEL

146

Step Ten: Screen the applicants and select your tenant-buyer.

Take the time to do your due diligence on your prospective tenant-buyers *after* they have committed to wanting the property. Protect your time.

Being able to properly screen a tenant-buyer before you allow them to move into one of your properties is an easy process and can help eliminate problems *before* they ever happen. I've met people who use their "gut feeling" to qualify their tenants. I've even talked to a fellow who "just knew" over the phone when he had a good tenant-buyer. We recommend that you do things differently.

First, create your own application that asks plenty of questions. Then charge an application fee to help weed out the people who will for some unknown reason fill out an application when they have no interest in purchasing from you. We charge $10 - $20 for each application per person who will be using his/her income to qualify for the property. If you charge a fee, then they will leave without filling out an application if they don't like the place. You now have an opportunity to find out why they didn't like it. If the rent is too high, or something else is wrong with your property, wouldn't you want to know about it?

The trick is to complete your checkout as fast as possible so that your *good* tenant-buyer doesn't get a call from some other landlord accepting him into another home before you have even processed his application.

There are four areas you will review when evaluating tenant-buyer applications: monthly income, credit history, past rental history, and option payment. If one or more of these four areas is weak, then the remaining areas need to be

147

strong enough to offset the weak one. Ideally, your tenant-buyer should have take-home income equal to at least three times the rent. Many tenant-buyers have credit problems, and this by itself should not stop you from choosing someone. Investigate if their credit report shows a history of not paying bills over a long period of time. See if one major event in the person's past caused major problems localized to one definite period of time. In most cases, a series of credit problems with small debtors is a big warning sign.

Without question, the single biggest factor in your review of a tenant-buyer's application is the size of the up-front option payment. The larger this option payment, the more security you have in the deal.

I can remember a three-bedroom home I had where my tenant-buyer had a past bankruptcy on his credit record. He had an accident that hurt his back and kept him from working for several months.

I knew this was a part of his credit history, but he also had $7,000 to work with as an option payment on the $115,000 property. He turned out to be a solid tenant-buyer and the deal was quite lucrative.

—DAVID FINKEL

Step Eleven: **Call and share the good news with your tenant-buyer.**

This is fun. Call up your tenant-buyer and share the good news. (Make sure to mention that you have a list of other people right there to call if they don't jump at the opportunity you are giving them.)

Step Twelve: **Meet with the tenant-buyer to complete the final paperwork and collect your money.**

You should use a separate lease contract and option to purchase contract with your tenant-buyer. The lease contract you use can be a standard rental agreement. The option contract must clearly state that their option to purchase is wholly dependent on being a good tenant-buyer and living up to all the terms of your lease contract.

Also, you will always collect the option payment and first month's rent before you ever allow a tenant-buyer to move into their new home. These two payments should be in certified funds such as a cashier's check or money order. By accepting this type of payment, you are protecting yourself.

[**Editor's Note**: To learn exactly what forms to fill out and how to put your tenant-buyer into one of your properties in the safest manner, see the Success Library in Appendix B for a list of resources.]

Now it's time to walk through some specific areas that will allow you to apply this system even more effectively. The result will be more time for you—and more money too! Do we have your interest? We thought so! Please keep reading.

How to Create a Ready Reserve of Hungry Tenant-Buyers

Are you ready to learn how to create a ready reserve of tenant-buyers? Let's face it, when you invest your money in classified ads or other lead generators to find tenant-buyers, you want to maximize your return on investment.

The way you do that is by turning all the calls you get

from your ad into a ready source of tenant-buyers for future properties. It probably seems like common sense to you, and it is, but so many investors either forget to do it or don't systematize it.

If you forget to collect names and numbers of potential tenant-buyers, you're throwing thousands of dollars away. If you fail to use a system, you are doomed to waste your valuable time and let potential profits slip away from you.

The solution is to create a prospective tenant-buyer database, keeping all the information in one place. You may want to include the following information:

- Name
- Address
- Phone Number
- Type of home they are looking for
- Preferred location
- Option payment they have to work with
- Monthly payment range
- Annual income of each person in household contributing to rent
- Next step

How to Pre-Program Your Prospective Tenant-Buyers to Buy Now!

Let's talk about how you pre-program your prospective tenant-buyers to quickly grab your offer. It's simply a matter of how you handle the tenant-buyer leads received through your voice mail.

As you are finding and qualifying people from your voice mail leads, touch base with them on the phone or in person, if they are at the property. Let them know you have a number of properties that come up on a regular basis. Programming them to buy quickly is step one.

Step two is telling someone that another person got the property. This call reinforces just how fast these properties go. The implicit message is that they need to act quickly or you will choose someone else for the property and they will miss out. Here's an example of how you can do that.

Just ask them:

"Would you like me to call you as soon as I have a property that meets your needs? This house that you just looked at went really fast. In fact, it just came up two days ago. I know that you looked at it today but someone who submitted their paperwork yesterday was actually approved by the office today."

A message like this instills in their mind that they need to move quickly to take advantage of the next rent to own home you show them. This technique is a simple way to pre-program your prospective tenant-buyers to jump quickly. The next time you call them with a property, they will know that they need to make a decision and move on it. A ready reserve of tenant-buyers will help you fill your properties fast.

How to Side-Step the Landlord Trap

I spent the first few years of my investing career finding and buying properties I could get into for little or nothing down. Many of these had been neglected by the owners and were in desperate need of fix-up and repair.

With each new property I bought, came the increased responsibilities of doing the fix-up work, handling routine maintenance and repairs, and dealing with tenant demands.

Even though I got to a point where I hired other people to do the work, I still had to look after their work, making sure it had been done properly, and was billed correctly. At one point I realized I was so busy managing the properties I owned, I hadn't bought a new property in over two years!

—PETER CONTI

Peter had fallen into the "Landlord Trap". He was in a position where his ability to invest in more properties had come to a standstill. "Free time" was the extra 30 minutes he had waiting for the plumber to show up. His young kids were beginning to grow up without him. It was probably Peter's intense dedication to his wife and family that drove him to develop a better way to invest both for himself and now for you. Out of every adversity comes tremendous change.

The one distinction that makes Purchase Option investing better than other real estate wealth-creation systems is:

You don't have to do any repairs, maintenance, or fix-up work ever again.

This concept is valuable to you because Purchase Option investors make more money than most "fix-em-up" investors. As a smart investor, you make your biggest profits when you buy or sell a property. When you stop buying and selling properties to pick up a hammer or paintbrush, your income drops.

Once you fully understand this concept, you'll never want

to pick up a hammer or a paintbrush again. Why would you, when you have a choice of making more than twice as much by working with the most powerful money making tool ever—the pen?

Purchase Option investing allows you to invest using merely a pen because of these two facts:

1. **Owners are responsible for the maintenance of their home.**
2. **Renters often expect *you* to fix what *they* break.**

Many ordinary "renters" tend to care less about your property because they don't have any future interest in the home. They are just living there for the time being and have no real incentive to maintain the property like an owner does.

Owners on the other hand, can be seen in any nice area on a Saturday morning fixing, maintaining, and upgrading their homes. Because you'll be putting a "tenant-buyer" into the home (using the rent to own concept), you'll have an occupant who is going to treat the home like his own. After all, he will own the home someday.

You are then able to escape the "Landlord Trap" because your tenant-buyer is going to take care of the minor fix-ups and maintenance each month. (These are the tasks that drive "old school" investors crazy.) To be fair to the tenant-buyer, you'll only have them take care of the first $200 in repairs each month.

It's surprising how much longer things last when your tenant knows that they are going to have to pay for something themselves when they break it!

—DAVID FINKEL

153

When you discuss this with your tenant-buyer, it will sound like this:

Mr. and Mrs. Tenant-Buyer, since you have the opportunity to buy this house, we will trust that you'll treat it just like you own it. Therefore, we will expect that you'll take care of any repairs that cost less than $200.00 per month. If something costs more than that, as long as you've provided us with several bids, we'll see to it that the amounts above the first $200 are covered.

Why You Won't Need to Pay for Major Repairs— Ever!

As part of your negotiations with your motivated sellers, you are going to arrange for them to cover any repairs over $200 that are needed while you are leasing the property from them. You'll find this simple and easy to do.

Mr. and Mrs. Seller, I know that you would like this home to be as much of a hands-free investment as possible. Keeping that in mind, I've arranged to take care of all the day-to-day maintenance.

To be fair, I'll take care of the first $200 of maintenance each month. This should cover just about everything. Does that sound fair to you?

The answer is almost always, "Yes". In the event that the seller doesn't want any responsibility at all for the property, what you'll do is simply arrange to purchase a "Home Warranty Policy". This is an insurance policy designed to cover the cost of major repairs. These policies vary in cost but should be in the range of $300 to $500 in most cases.

(You may even be able to get the seller to pay for it.)

Let's look and see who is responsible for the maintenance when following the system.

Tenant-buyer — Pays first $200 in repairs each month.

Seller — Pays any amount over $200 each month.

You, the investor — Pay nothing in time or money and are free to pursue other moneymaking deals.

With this arrangement in place for multiple properties, you'll be able to enjoy the same position that many of our students do. You will have created multiple streams of income buying homes in nice areas with nothing down. By setting up your deals correctly, you'll be sitting back collecting money, having safely sidestepped the Landlord Trap.

"The People who get on in this
world are the people
who get up and look for
the circumstances they
want, and, if they can't find them,
make them.

—George Bernard Shaw

Section Five:

Seven Fun, Easy Ways to Make up to an Extra $100,000 This Year Investing in Real Estate

Purchase Option is a collection of new strategies for real estate investment that combines the best of the tried and true methods of the past with cutting edge techniques, resulting in the safest, most powerful investment system available.

The real beauty of Purchase Option is that you are able to control a property by making payments to a seller which are much lower than if you went out and bought the property with 100% financing.

By doing this you capture the benefits of real estate like:

- The appreciation of the property—bringing you long-term profits
- Increasingly larger monthly streams of cash-flow
- The equity paydown or amortization of the underlying loan on the property—this means that as the loan is paid down you make more money
- Safe leverage of your time and money—small investment of time and money create a huge return for you

And you'll get all of that without any of the downsides of traditional real estate investing like:

- Negative cash flow
- Maintenance hassles
- High risk because of the large down payment needed
- Need for good credit
- Headaches of dealing with banks and renters

This means you'll be able to avoid many of the pitfalls that await those using the "old school" investment methods, while enjoying big profits.

Low Risk

The first rule of investing is to control your losses. Sometimes the best decision you can make is to walk away from the deal. Just one bad deal can quickly eat up the profits from three or four good deals.

By using the Purchase Option techniques correctly, you can control your risk, limiting your losses from any one deal to the absolute minimum. Compared to other methods, you'll make higher profits because you get to keep what you make instead of losing three of every four dollars.

Maximum Safety

By working the Purchase Option system, you will keep your up-front investment in any property as close to zero as possible. Also, because you are never going to fully commit to a deal until you have a clear plan of how you will market the property, you'll minimize your risk in any deal.

Minimum Time Requirements

The biggest benefit of using the Purchase Option technique is you only have to work hard to get your deal put together (you pick your hours), then once it's done, the time required from you is next to nothing. You receive a rent check from your tenant-buyer. You deposit it in your bank account. You write a smaller check to your seller. Done. Many of our students like the ability to create multiple streams of income by working from their own home during the hours that they choose.

159

[**Editor's Note:** If you are serious about your financial future and would like to know exactly how you might be able to qualify to work one-on-one with Peter or David, call Mentor Financial Group, LLC at (303)233-2233 and ask to speak with Jamie. Each year Peter and David select a few special investors to mentor and teach exactly how to put the Purchase Option system to work creating massive wealth.]

The Benefits of Different Purchase Option Techniques:

1. Quick Cash

Making immediate cash has always been a priority for many investors. By using Purchase Option techniques you can create not only immediate streams of money that come to you each and every month, but also large chunks of quick cash from:

- Tenant buyer option payments
- The Quick-Cash Technique
- The Discount Purchase Option Technique

2. Cash-flow

Once your immediate financial needs are met, your life will become easier as multiple streams of income come in each and every month. Isn't the American dream really to have enough income so that you would never have to work another day in your life if you didn't want to? Purchase Option investing helps you to create monthly streams of cash-flow. And as you grow your portfolio of deals, you are also increasing your monthly passive income.

3. Long-term wealth building

Would you like to borrow a million dollars from a friend interest free for five years? Imagine you had a friend who said, "Here is the money. All I want is for you to return my original million dollars back to me within five years. Any profits you make with the money are yours to keep." Wouldn't you love to have a friend like that?

In a sense that's exactly what you're able to enjoy with Purchase Option investing. The only real difference is that instead of a million dollars cash earning you money, you have a million dollars worth of property that you control earning you money. Just like that million dollars sitting in a bank at five percent would earn you $50,000 a year, as the value of the real estate you control goes up in value, you are making money with someone else's asset! This is leveraging in the best sense.

When I first met my wife, I bragged a bit about my real estate investments. Of course I did. I would imagine that every person paints a pretty picture of himself when he meets someone he really likes. And when that person is as beautiful as my wife, well let's just say I wanted to impress her as much as I could.

Luckily for me my investments turned out even better than I had made them out to be. I remember the look in her eyes the first time I brought home a check for $77,000. It was a look of excited delight and admiration at the same time. Of course, by continuing to follow my own system, I am financially more successful and I continually feel the support and admiration of my wife and family.

–Peter Conti

Now that you are clear on the benefits of Purchase Option investing, let's work through seven different Purchase Option strategies.

Seven Powerful Purchase Option Techniques:

#1: The Lease Option

The lease option is the foundation of many Purchase Option techniques. This is the strategy you learned so much about in the earlier sections of this book. Still, let's take a moment to ensure you are clear on this technique's basic elements before we advance to the others.

The components of the lease option are:

- A lease of at least two years time
- An option to buy at today's value or lower
- Rent at or below area market rent

The lease option is an incredibly powerful tool. This method alone will allow you to control real estate in a way that creates wealth without risk. The best part is that you can set it up so your tenant-buyer takes care of the maintenance for you. You sit in the middle just like a banker — with little risk and lots of profit!

The Golden Rule of All Your Offers

Always use an offer form that includes a "subject to" clause. (An offer form approved by your attorney is safest)

In all the offers you make, you are going to insert a "subject to" clause. This means that your offer is contingent upon some other factor such as a final inspection, or a partner's approval. It isn't so important what the condition is, as long as it allows you to tie up a property, while at the same time have an escape hatch from the deal.

This allows you to quickly sort through sellers to find a deal, then to lock up that deal as fast as possible before any other investors snap it up for themselves. Once you have the deal under contract, you go out and do your due diligence.

Of course, you will treat the seller with respect, and make your final decision about the property within a reasonable period of time. Usually, this means giving the seller a final answer within a few weeks. Whenever you use a "subject to" clause, you need to act with integrity to be fair to both you and the seller.

One of the best parts about the lease option is that many times you can make money even if you pay today's full price and current market rent for a property. This is because in most markets, the future appreciation of the property will let you build in a healthy back-end profit. (Just make sure you negotiate a longer lease option term to compensate for the higher price you might have agreed to pay.)

The problem with making full price offers is like the time I sold my 1965 Oldsmobile. It was a decent car that ran well and looked good. It was just older than most other cars. I ran an ad in the paper advertising it for $500. The morning the ad came out I received three calls and the first person who came out plunked $500 down on the hood and drove off. I was left standing there wondering if I could have gotten more.

—PETER CONTI

The point is this: Negotiation serves a purpose beyond just trying to get the best deal for yourself. It also helps to bind the other party to follow through with the agreement. People feel more committed if they had to work a little bit to get you to agree to a deal. Even if you end up giving the owner full asking price, he realizes you are profit oriented and will be more comfortable with you.

Don't offer too much, too soon. If you do and they accept your offer, they will immediately begin to wonder how you are going to make any money. They will become confused, and since a confused mind always says, "No," they will begin to undo the great deal you just put together.

There is an added benefit that after some back and forth negotiation, you just might end up with a more profitable deal. Once you get good at putting together the lease option, you can move on to some of the more advanced techniques.

#2: The Equity-Split

When searching for motivated sellers, you'll find that some of them are more motivated than others. We used to bypass sellers who had some motivation but didn't want to give up all of the future appreciation of their property. Now you can make money even with sellers who are only somewhat motivated by using the Equity-Split technique.

The Equity-Split strategy is a way for you to "partner" up with the seller of the property. What you do is agree on the terms of a normal lease option with one added element. This added element is an up-front agreement to share the profits made when you resell the property for a higher price than the option price you agreed to pay your seller. You can negotiate this future profit split any way you want (e.g. 50%-50%, 35%-65%, etc.)

164

Because you are sharing future profits in the deal with the seller, you will need a longer term on an equity split so that you have more potential profits in the deal. This is easier to negotiate since the seller is, in a very real way, your partner and the more money you make, the more money he will make. Also, you shouldn't have to give the seller any up-front money since he is your partner. And in many cases, a seller who is doing an equity split with you will be willing to cover a negative cash-flow on the property because of the future profits he stands to make.

The real benefit to the seller in an equity split is that his immediate problems with his property are solved. He also limits his risk since you are guaranteeing him a monthly payment. You are also taking care of all the day-to-day maintenance for him, and he gets to keep all the tax benefits of owning the property until the time your tenant-buyer purchases. Because you have agreed to split the profits with him, he gets to benefit from the future appreciation of the home. Not bad for a hands-off, passive investment for the seller.

Example: Ellen, an investor, meets with a motivated seller, Mike. After talking for a while, Ellen finds out that Mike's motivation for selling is to move into a larger home because his family is growing. But Mike is not in a big hurry to sell. The worst case for him is that he could rent out the house and sell after a few years. The house is worth $175,000 and has a market rental value of $1,275.

Ellen drew out of Mike that he wasn't thrilled with the idea of being a landlord. Mike was a successful professional who earned a healthy income and felt his free time with his family would suffer if he had to manage the house as a rental property. Mike's major objection to doing a lease-option with Ellen was that he was not motivated enough to give up the future appreciation of the home if he wasn't getting cashed out right away.

Ellen quickly switched gears and asked Mike whether he would be interested if there was a way for him to turn the property into a hands-off, passive investment where he would still get all the tax benefits of owning the property, and get a large chunk of the future appreciation of the property, without having to do any work. As you can imagine, Mike was excited about this.

Here's what they agreed to:

A lease-option on the property with the following terms:

- Rent: $1,200/month
- Price: $171,000
- Term: 6 Years

They also agreed that when Ellen's tenant-buyer bought the property, Ellen and Mike would split any amount over $171,000. They agreed to split this profit with 40% going to Mike and 60% going to Ellen. Of course, since Ellen was responsible for looking after the property and had even guaranteed Mike monthly payments, she got to keep all the cash-flow from the property.

Three years later, Ellen's tenant-buyer purchased the property for $205,000. $171,000 went to Mike and the remaining $34,000 profit was split between Ellen and Mike with Ellen getting $20,400 and Mike getting $13,600. The cash-flow Ellen had made on the property was hers to keep. After all, she was the one responsible for the property's oversight. (Of course, since she used the Purchase Option strategies you are learning about, her tenant-buyer took care of all the day-to-day maintenance and gave Ellen $10,000 up-front as an option payment.)

To put together an Equity Split Purchase Option you'll want:

A lease option term of at least four years. (so the long-term profits are large enough to share with the owner.)
A fair split of the deal's future profits with the owner.

The Equity Split technique is used to give you a reasonable monthly cash flow while sharing the long term profits with the seller. You will have full control over the property just as you do in a lease option. The biggest difference is that the owner will receive a percentage of the profits at the time you sell the property.

#3: The Cash-Flow Technique

We have to thank our students for helping us to constantly upgrade the quality and variety of the strategies and techniques we share with people. Because they continually bring new situations to us for help in putting together deals, we see thousands of potential deals every year, adding to the information base we provide to investors like you. The Cash-Flow technique is one such strategy that was born from a deal found by two of our students.

Here's a story about a seller that two of my students, Jim and Margaret, went out to visit with me who turned out to be a perfect candidate for the Cash-Flow technique.

We were navigating our way through the posh neighborhood following the directions that Margaret had written down. She was sitting in the front next to me, and Jim was in the back gathering up the camera and notepad to take into the property.

We knocked at the door and were greeted by Sarah, a petite woman who looked to be about 50. She was wearing a pair of old jeans and a worn sweater. She apologized, saying that she had to do the cleaning today because her help hadn't shown up. The house was even nicer on the inside than the rose garden suggested from the outside. I felt like I was looking through one of the houses I had seen in a magazine. White tile floors with blue accents matched the furniture and accessories. Blue glass place settings on the dining room table made it look as if we had arrived just in time for a formal dinner party.

Sarah walked us through the house, showing off everything from the jacuzzi tub in the master bath to a luxurious office overlooking the living room from above. I kept thinking, "Yes! This is nice."

The view of fields out the back were impressive and the kitchen was fit for a master chef. We were making our way out to the pool by walking through the greenhouse when I asked Sarah about her motivation.

"With such a beautiful house why would you ever consider selling?" I asked.

Sarah's tone dropped as she replied, "I run a cleaning business and one of my employees was hurt on the job. I didn't have workman's compensation insurance so now I can't afford to make my house payments." The pain was evident in her voice although I was impressed with her ability to hold her head up in such trying circumstances.

We continued into the back yard and found another hot tub by the pool, a huge storage area for an RV, and an orchard containing two hundred exotic fruit trees.

Back inside, the three of us sat down at the kitchen table. Sarah explained that her monthly payments were $2200. This was a small payment for a house of this value because she had put a tidy sum down when she bought the property. She went on to explain how she had put an additional $50,000 into home improvements. The house was in mint condition.

"I won't accept a penny less than $500,000." Sarah said. Our research showed that the house was worth a little less than this but it was a situation where the cash-flow technique works so well.

This was a nice house in a nice area, in mint condition, with a motivated seller, and low payments. Everything needed to make an incredible deal was present and I was eager to put it together. We felt that the property could be rented out for $3,600 to $3,900 a month!

Sarah accepted an offer from us to lease her house over the next five years for $2,600 a month with an option to buy it for $500,000. Margaret and Jim were thrilled. I was pretty excited too. We realized that even if the property never appreciated enough to allow us to resell it at a price higher than the inflated $500,000 figure Sarah insisted on, we would still be making over $1,000 a month in cash-flow from the property!

And at the end of five years we could choose not to exercise our option to purchase the property. Remember, with the Purchase Option techniques you have the option to purchase, not the obligation.

In the event we didn't buy the place after five years, Sarah would still win. We would have covered her payments for five years in a way where she made a $400 profit on the property each month. She would have gotten all the tax benefits of owning the property, while we would handle all the day to day maintenance. Everybody was thrilled when we left Sarah that day. It was a real win-win.

—Peter Conti

With this technique, you can generate enough cash flow from the property to make a substantial profit. You are even willing to agree to an inflated option price in return for a lower rent and longer term for you to control the property.

#4: Owner Carry Technique

At some point in your investing career, you are sure to meet with a seller who owns a property free and clear. When you do, remember the Owner Carry technique where you give a seller a small down payment, then make monthly payments to him for the balance.

Of course, since you will be collecting 3-5% of the home's value as an option payment from your tenant-buyer, this is the money you will use as your down payment to the seller. This is an extremely powerful technique that combines traditional owner carry finance with the concept of using a tenant-buyer's money. The result is a nothing down deal with thousands in profits for you.

REMEMBER: Nothing down does not mean the seller gets no money down… It means that you don't have to put any of your own money down!

Note: Structure the deal so that you do not pay the seller any money until you collect your option payment from the tenant-buyer.

#5: The Big Money Cash Close

If you meet with a seller who has a large chunk of equity in their property but who is not open to one of the other purchase option techniques, then you can use the Big Money Cash close. This technique allows you to offer the seller up to 60% of the value of the home in cash at closing if he is willing to carry the balance as a second mortgage.

Before you worry about where you are going to come up with that kind of cash, know that it won't be *your* money.

For example, Sam owns a $100,000 home with a first mortgage of $15,000 owed against the property. You offer to bring in new financing and give Sam $60,000 at closing if he is willing to carry back a small second mortgage for the remaining $40,000. This means that at closing Sam will get $15,000 to pay off the old first mortgage and $45,000 to put in his pocket. You negotiate the terms of the remaining $40,000 second mortgage. Typically this is done with a 5-7 year balloon note with interest only payments.

Where do you get the $60,000 to give Sam at closing? You simply go out and get a new first mortgage on the property for $60,000. Since the loan is for less than 60% of the value of the property you can usually get a non-qualifying loan. After all, since the lender is only lending up to 60% of the value of the property, its loan is well secured.

Then you simply put your tenant-buyer in the property to cover the payments and cash you out of the property in a few years.

#6: Quick-Cash Technique

The Quick-Cash technique is a way for you to cash out of your deals fast—within 60 days or less! What you'll do is find a person to buy out your contract on the property.

The basic ingredients of this technique are:

Having a locked-in deal using one of the other purchase option strategies

Having an assignable contract

"Flipping" your agreement to another party

The Quick-Cash technique is your way to create an immediate payday from your deals. In essence, what you are doing is selling your position in the deal to another party. This is commonly called "flipping" your contract.

Typically when you do this, you can capture between 25-50% of the total locked-in profits up front from the other party. Then you use a simple assignment form to assign your interest over to that other party.

There are two groups you can sell your deal to:

1. Another Investor

Try bringing the deal to your local REIA meeting—Real Estate Investors Association. Chances are there is another investor who would love to buy your deal from you because he knows that the payoff down the road gives him a great return on his money. [**Editor's note:** For a free listing of real estate investor groups in your area go to www.resultsnow.com]

2. Your tenant-buyer

You'll be surprised at how resourceful tenant-buyers can be when they have the chance to secure a lower monthly rent and price and a longer term simply by coming up with some more up-front money.

Whenever I put a tenant-buyer into a property who has given me a large down payment I always consider using the quick cash technique. It's so easy to use. I simply ask my tenant-buyer if they have any interest in getting a lower price and rent if they could come up with a larger up-front payment. This cashes me out faster and gives my tenant-buyer an even better deal.

—DAVID FINKEL

#7: The Discount Technique

Sellers of property like to get cash quickly just like you do. You're going to use this to your advantage with the Discount Purchase Option Technique.

Here's an example of how to use this technique:

You've set up a Purchase Option deal using perhaps the Lease Option technique. The seller of the property knows it may take up to 6 years to get paid off in full. You, however, have a tenant-buyer in the property one or two years into the deal. You make a simple phone call to the seller that is going to make you some big money. Here's what it should sound like:

"Hello, Mr. Seller? It's Jill Investor, the one that sends you that rent check each and every month. I know that we had talked about me buying your property at the end of 6 years, but an unusual situation has come up, and you may want to take advantage of it. You see, I'll be getting a lump sum of money soon from another source [your tenant-buyer] and I thought it might make sense, if you were willing to give me a discount, for me to pay you off now rather than wait until the end of the six years. Are you interested in getting most of your money right away or would you rather wait until the end of the six years for me to cash you out? How much of a discount are you willing to give me?"

It's pretty clear how this technique is going to allow you to convert a great deal into an outstanding one. Each time I've used this technique, I'm surprised at how easy it is. The last time I used it I made an extra $10,000. That's pretty good pay for a five minute phone call.

—PETER CONTI

If the seller says "No, I'm happy just waiting for my money," then you, of course, will go ahead and allow your tenant-buyer to purchase the home. Just make sure you call using this script—first—to see if the seller will take your great offer. It can't hurt, and most likely you'll end up making at least a few thousand extra dollars of profit for the effort of your five minute phone call!

This is why you should build a relationship with a mortgage lender in your area who you can hook up with your tenant-buyer. When the lender helps your tenant-buyer qualify for a loan faster, the lender makes money, your tenant-buyer gets to own a home sooner, the seller will get cashed out faster, and you stand to win big too. You'll make more money—faster! This is win-win investing at its best.

Many times what you will be doing is layering one purchase option technique onto another to build more profits into the deal for yourself. For instance, every time your tenant-buyer is ready to purchase, you will go back to the seller and use the discount purchase option technique. Or you can have a basic lease option deal that moves into an owner-carry deal based on the seller having received a year or two of consistent payments from you. Any one of these techniques by itself is powerful, but when you combine them you take your investing to the next level.

Bonus Technique!

#8: The Master Lease Option

A Technique to Buy Apartment Buildings With Nothing Down

To use the Master Lease Option technique you'll need to take three steps.

Step one is the same as buying a nice home with nothing down: find a motivated seller who has a specific need or problem for you to solve and who will be open to your creative offer.

I heard about Carrie from a real estate agent named Tim with whom I had an established relationship. Tim was out fishing for listings when he found a 24-unit apartment building, owned by a woman named Carrie, who needed some help.

Carrie had worked hard all of her adult life managing the 24-unit apartment building she owned. She cleaned, fixed, and rented the units over the years, expecting the building to support her in her old age.

What an unpleasant surprise it was for Carrie and her family to find that it didn't work out that way, even though she owned the building free and clear. At the time Tim, the real estate agent, heard about her, she was 88 years old and living in California with her children. She was diagnosed with Alzheimer's disease and needed to go into a nursing home where she could receive special care. This care cost $3,000 a month.

The problem was her apartment building wasn't producing enough money to pay for her nursing home. Despite hiring three different management companies in the past three years, the building was only making about $2,000 a month after paying the management company and all of the expenses.

Tim offered to list the property for Carrie's Trust, which was how the property was set up, due to Carrie's declining health. Her kids didn't want to sell the property outright because a large part of the money from the sale would have to go toward paying capital gains tax. Tim called me because he knew that I was always looking for situations where property owners were motivated and he knew he was unable to help Carrie himself. (I send Tim properties that don't work for a creative, nothing down offer but that might work great for a listing and direct sale for him)

—PETER CONTI

Step two is to "run the numbers" to see if you'll make a profit. You'll want to know with certainty that any property you get into is going to make you, not cost you, money. The best time to find this out is before you commit to a deal.

I looked closely at the income and expenses from the building to see if there was any way to improve the cash flow. I knew right away that because the management fees were close to $1,000 a month I could pay Carrie the $3,000 a month she needed and still break even. The question was, could I make a profit?

The rents seemed to be low which meant that there was room to increase the cash flow after taking control of the property. I used a software program I had developed called the "Property Cash Flow Evaluator" to allow me to determine the first year's cash flow from the property. The numbers showed this to be a winning deal.

—PETER CONTI

[**Editors Note**: To download your free copy of the "Property Cash Flow Evaluator" software program used to evaluate this apartment building and other income properties simply visit www.resultsnow.com]

Step three is creating an offer that uses the cash flow from the property to pay for the deal.

I offered Carrie's Trust a "master lease" that would meet her needs and allow me to make a profit too. In return for our monthly payment of $3,000 and paying for all the expenses on the property, I received the exclusive option to purchase the building for $450,000, which was it's current value based on its rental income. I simply used the income from the property to pay for both the expenses and the lease payment to Carrie's Trust.

I immediately began lowering expenses and increasing rents. Rather than increasing everyone's rent at once, I sent notices to 1/3 of the building each month for three months. Some tenants moved while others complained a bit about the rent increase but decided to stay. Most just paid the increased amount and were fine with it.

Within four months of taking over the building, raising rents to market levels and lowering expenses, I was able to increase the cash-flow an average of $85 per unit. This boosted the total monthly income from $7,100 to $9,182.

This was a monthly cash flow increase of $2,082. I was thrilled to create an annual residual income of $24,987.

And this amount would grow every year as the rents increased over time. This is as much money from one property as many people work all year to make.

This made me even more money than just the cash-flow each month. Income property is valued in proportion to the amount of income it generates each year. When valuing an income property, you use something called a "capitalization rate" or "cap rate." In its simplest form, since the average cap rate is 10, this means a building is valued at 10 times the amount of its annual cash-flow.

This means that the annual increase in cash flow of $24,987 made my building worth $249,870 more than it was worth just four months before. How's that for an additional profit center?

—Peter Conti

The nice thing about great cash flow like this is that you can afford to hire a property management company while you sit back and wait for the property to go up in value. That's exactly what Peter did, and you can too, if you follow the three steps of the Master Lease Option.

First, find a motivated seller who owns a multi-unit building. Next, run the numbers to make certain you'll make money each month if you were to lease out the property with the option to purchase. Finally, create an offer that uses the cash flow from the property to cover your monthly payments and expenses. Then increase the property's value by lowering expenses and increasing the money it generates.

One of the buildings I bought using the Master Lease Option has generated over $350,000 in locked-in profits! Not to mention a five figure annual cash-flow.

—Peter Conti

A Quick Review of Purchase Option Techniques

Purchase Option Techniques

Technique	Advantages	Disadvantages	Payoff
Basic Purchase Option	– Easiest technique to get started with. – Little time after property is set up. – Low-risk and large profit potential. – Can be set up with nothing down.	– Requires effort to put together. – Up to 2/3 of money comes after 2 to 3 years. – Requires mentor to learn rapidly.	– Monthly cash flow. – Up-front option payment. – Long term wealth buildup.
Equity Split Purchase Option	– Works well with less than motivated seller. – Little time after property is set up. – Low risk and large profit potential. – Can be set up with nothing down.	– Long-term profits are split with the seller. – Requires effort to put together. – Up to 2/3 of profit comes after 2 to 3 years.	– Monthly cash flow. – Up-front option payment. – Half of long term wealth buildup.
Quick Cash Purchase Option	– Allows you to walk away from the deal with cash. – No Long-term commitment. – Creates quick cash. – Possible to do with nothing down.	– Larger option payment required from tenant buyer. – Makes less money overall compared to long term techniques.	– Lump sum of cash up front. – No time needed after assigned.
Discount Purchase Option	– Turns a good deal into a great deal. – Easy to implement. – Makes you more money than you expected. – No risk.	– Seller won't always give a discount.	– A larger chunk of money than you were expecting because seller discounts price.

Owner Carry Purchase Option	– Allows owner to "sell" rather than lease. – No banks to deal with. – Often able to negotiate below market interest rates.	– Seller often wants money down. – Harder to structure deal to get positive cash-flow than basic lease option.	– Massive long-term wealth build-up. – Investor gets tax benefits of property. – Investor on title—provides added security in deal.
Cash-Flow Purchase Option	– Creates residual monthly income. – Allows investor to offer seller higher price. – Little risk.	– Often investor must agree to a higher option price which means less long-term profit from resale of property. – Requires effort up-front to set up.	– Large monthly streams of income. – Up-front option payment. – Some long term wealth buildup.
Big Money Cash Close Purchase Option	– Allows owner to "sell" rather than lease. – Seller gets big chuck of cash up-front. – Still nothing down deal for investor.	– Investor may have to sign personally on note to get new first mortgage. – Have to deal with a bank—red tape.	– Now able to buy property that "lease option" only investors can't. – Massive long-term wealth build-up. – Investor gets tax benefits.
Master Lease Purchase Option	– Can be used to create wealth on a large sacle. – No banks required. – Can buy apartment buildings with nothing down.	– Extremely time itensive in the beginning stages. – May want to hire a property management company.	– Monthly cash flow. – Massive long-term wealth build-up.

181

Section Six:

How to Find, Close, And Structure Money-Making Purchase Option Deals

Real Life Examples of How Other
Investors Have Done It
(And *How* You Can Too!)

Case Study #1: Dan's First Deal

Case study number one is a small deal, but an important one. It's important because it was our student Dan's first. After he completed this deal, Dan knew that making money with real estate wasn't just possible—it was possible for him.

Dan found his motivated sellers by calling through aged classified ads. The sellers had tried to sell the house on their own for several months unsuccessfully. Dan called them using a "for sale" classified ad he found in his local daily paper that he had aged approximately six weeks.

The sellers were a nice family who had outgrown this house (a 3 bedroom, 2 bath, 2 car garage home) and had built a new home nearby. Their problem was that they were not able to sell their old house. And unless they did, due to the unaffordable double payments, they would lose the financing on their new home.

Dan stepped in and locked up an eight-year lease option on the house covering the seller's payments of $800 a month. Dan offered them full market value for their house—$103,874.

Dan marketed the property in two ways. First, he put a small "Rent to Own" classified ad in the "for sale" section of his local paper. Second, he put up a large "Rent to Own" sign in the front yard of the house. These two simple steps flooded his voice mail box with queries from potential tenant-buyers.

He set up two group showings for the home and found his tenant-buyers —a young couple who were about to have their first baby. This family was thrilled to be able to "rent to own" the house on a two year term with a monthly rent of $850 and a purchase price of $116,518. For them, this meant they could stop renting and start owning before their first child was born. Everyone was thrilled. Especially Dan. (See chart 7 on page 186)

Dan had $13,844 of locked-in profits in the deal. Again, while this was not a big deal, it was Dan's first and that makes this deal important. Maybe your first deal will have profits of only $10,000 to $15,000. That's OK, because the important thing is to get your first deal done. There is no better way to learn than by doing.

Listen to Dan as he shares how he felt about his first deal.

My tenant-buyer just left and I can't believe how easy it is to make money with Purchase Option investing. The seller was thrilled that I would take over her payments and the tenant-buyers were excited to get into a purchase option so easily.

I used the agreement forms and just filled in the blanks like you told me to. I've spent more time filling out the forms to buy a car than I did writing up this deal.

Total profits from my first Purchase Option deal are $13,844. I just added up the hours putting this together and I don't even have eight hours invested. I'll let you do the math, but I'm fairly certain that this pays better than my $7.70 an hour job at the ski shop.

—DAN HARRIGAN

Motivated Seller		Hungry Tenant-Buyer
	$50/month	
$800	**Rent**	$850
	$12,644	
$103,874	**Price**	$116,518
8 Years	**Term**	2 Years
$10	**Pymt**	$3,000

Total Profits:

24 months x $50/month = $1,200
Plus spread in prices = $12,644
_____

$13,844

Chart 7

Case Study #2 and #3

The following comes from a letter sent to us from Craig and Susan, two of our students investing in Colorado. Craig is a commercial airline pilot for one of the major airlines and Susan is a homemaker. They got started using the Purchase Option system because they wanted to earn the money to put their two sons through college.

Dear Peter,

Here are the details of the two deals we've done after attending your 3-day intensive training in June:

Deal 1:

We placed an "I buy houses" ad in our local paper. The seller responded to the ad by calling the 24- hour voice mail number. The voice mail used David's scripted message which got the seller to qualify himself in terms of motivation on a scale of one through ten [ten being incredibly motivated]. The seller rated himself as a "9."

When I called the seller back, he was very motivated. He wanted to get out from under the burden of the house payments and expenses. He had lost control of his finances and was deeply in debt. All he wanted was to be able to pay off his debts and start over financially. (He planned on just moving in with a friend.)

He had first tried to sell the house himself for $151,000 by advertising it in the local For Sale By Owner magazine. When this didn't work, he lowered the price to $149,900.

He then tried to sell it for $139,900 by putting out a "For

Sale" sign with some flyers in the front yard. He didn't have much luck.

By the time he and I talked he was really motivated. He told me he was willing to give me $5,000 to get rid of the house.

Here are the financial details on the house:

Value of the house: $141,500
First mortgage balance: $118,000
Second mortgage balance: $ 21,000

Seller's Equity: $2,500

Payment on the first mortgage: $1,040
Payment on the second mortgage: $ 300

Seller's Total Monthly Payment $1,340

On August 15, we agreed to a three-year lease option on the house. I would pay him a monthly rent of $1,040 (the amount of his first mortgage payment) and he would pay the monthly $300 second mortgage payment himself. My option price was for the balance of the mortgages [$139,000.]

The seller paid me $2,000 to do the deal. The $2,000 was to cover my monthly negative cash-flow and to do some repairs to the house. In the end all it cost me to fix up the house was about $200 for a thorough cleaning.

I took possession of the house on October 1, but my first payment was not due until November 1. [This meant Craig got to pocket the October rent payment he collected from his tenant-buyer of $995 as extra profit.]

I then put an ad in the Longmont newspaper, offering the house as a "Rent to Own" for $995/month. The ad directed readers to a voice mail box that gave all the details of the house, the offer, and the address. The tenant-buyer would have the option to buy the house anytime during the 12-month lease period for $152,900 and would need a non-refundable option payment of $3,000. Rent credits and down payment assistance were offered if the prospective tenant-buyer wanted to pay extra each month. The voice mail asked them to check out the neighborhood and the outside of the house first, then to call my direct phone number if they were seriously interested. [Craig's direct phone number was on an application packet he had attached to a sign in front of the house.]

About 10 people called me direct, with three who were really serious. The person who we eventually chose was a man in the middle of a divorce. He wanted to lease out the home for a short period, and then once the divorce was final he wanted to buy it.

Here's exactly what he paid me to get into the property:

First month's rent: $ 995
Security deposit: $ 500
Option payment: $3,000
Application Fee: $ 25

Total money he paid up-front: $4,520

My tenant-buyer told me he intends to exercise his option to purchase in the next four months. When he does, I will make an additional $9,400.

My total profits will be the sum of the $2,000 I collected from the seller, $4,520 I got from my tenant-buyer upfront, and the $9,400 I'll get at the closing when my tenant-buyer buys. Expenses will be about $1,500, so my net profits will be $14,420. Not bad for a first deal.

Deal 2:

This house was advertised as a "FSBO" [For Sale By Owner] in the local paper. When Susan [Craig's wife] called, they were willing to consider a lease option.

I went to visit them and see the house. Their real need was for me to cover their payment so they could qualify for a new loan in the city where they were being transferred.

Financial Details:

Value of house: $139,000
First mortgage: $114,000
Second mortgage: $ 16,000

Seller's Equity: $9,000

Payment on first mortgage: $1,028
Payment on second mortgage: $ 200
Total monthly payment: $1,228

The market rent for this house was about $1,200. The seller and I negotiated a three year lease option with a monthly rent of $1,100 [again notice Craig got the seller to agree to cover $128 a month of negative cash-flow.] My option price is $136,000. My occupancy begins on October 1, but my first payment is not due until November 1.

—Craig Johnson

190

Craig and Susan went on to market this house as a rent to own and made just under $15,000 profit. Again, we wanted to emphasize that both Dan's first deal and Craig and Susan's first two deals were small ones. And that is often how things work out. As you get more comfortable working the system, you will find yourself making more and more money on each deal.

In the beginning, I was just thrilled to make $3,000 quickly flipping one of my deals to another investor. But nowadays I find that the deals I make have much larger profits. For example, one of my tenant-buyers just purchased one of my properties and I collected a $51,000 check at the closing table. You'll find the same thing happening for you. Your profits will keep getting bigger and bigger as you grow more and more confident.

—PETER CONTI

Craig and Susan found the exact same thing to be true. Here's a look at what they did on their fourth deal.

Case Study #4

Craig and Susan have gotten real good at dividing up their investing work. Susan spends a few hours a day on the telephone calling up property owners. When she finds a motivated seller who has a situation that fits, she sets up an appointment for Craig to go out and visit with the owner. When Craig meets with the seller, Craig simply listens to the seller and his situation and figures out how he can help him. Finding deals really is this simple: you spend a few hours making phone calls, set up a few appointments, and find a seller you can really help. It takes a bit of work, but the format is simple.

Susan found our next case study by calling a property owner who advertised a house for rent in the local real estate classified ads. She called up the owner and used the Quick-Check script you learned about in this book.

When she found out that the owner had some motivation, Susan set up an appointment for Craig to go out and see the house.

Craig and Susan locked up a six-year lease option with the motivated seller with rent of $1,402 and a price of $170,200 (several thousand dollars below market value.) Then they advertised the property as a "rent to own" and found their tenant-buyer within a few weeks. They have $193 a month positive cash-flow on the property. (See chart 8 on page 193)

Their total profits from this deal will be over $40,000. Craig and Susan did ten deals in their first year of working the Purchase Option system part-time. If they can do it, so can you!

Motivated Seller   Hungry Tenant-Buyer

$193/month

$1402 $1595

| **Rent** |

$37,014

$170,200 $207,214

| **Price** |

6 Years   3 Years

| **Term** |

$3000 $6,000

| **Pymt** |

Total Profits:

36 months x $193/month = $ 6,948
Plus spread in prices   = $37,014
                                              ――――――――――
                                                $43,962

Chart 8

Case Study #5: Betty's First Deal

Our fifth case study property is a 3 bedroom, 2 bath, 2 car garage house in Colorado. The seller owned a lot of trailers that she rented out, and she wanted to live in her RV full time and phase out of the rental business.

Our student, Betty, sent us a letter describing how she put this deal together:

I haven't been trying that hard. I just made a list of about 40 numbers from an old May 12th paper. I called through that list a couple of times over two weeks time, contacting about a total of 10-15 property owners. Of these, I made appointments with two.

They didn't lead to any deals but they left me with some really good contacts – one with a mortgage broker and one with a law firm employee.

Next, I called the "For Sale By Owners" in my neighborhood and made one appointment. The seller did not seem to be motivated but I left her with an Initial Offer Form.

She called me back about a week later and asked me to sign her up. She felt that since I was a neighbor, she could trust me and also liked that I was nearby to watch over her property. She totally understood what she was doing and what the contract was all about, which was important to me, since I need to know that what I'm doing is honest and ethical.

—BETTY COLLINS

Betty signed a six-year lease-option with the seller. She went on to find her tenant-buyer via her super-response ad in her local paper. Of course, the ad led into her voice mail box which had the scripted message she got from our program, detailing all the benefits her prospective tenant-buyers would find irresistible.

In the end, she selected her tenant-buyers, and collected $10,000 as their up-front, non-refundable option payment. All totaled, Betty has $30,000 of locked-in profits in this deal.

In her letter to our office, Betty went on to say:

It's been fun! My goodness, I didn't really think I could do this so easily. But I did and I'm really psyched! My self-esteem is higher than it has been since I was two years old. I thank you both for it and look forward to doing more deals...

The biggest benefit I received by going to your 3 day intensive training was getting to know the people behind the books that I had read. And knowing that someone really was doing this for a living. And of course, the actual dialing and going out on appointments we did really allowed me to feel how "doable" this was. The ultimate benefit I received in the long run was a new career!

—BETTY COLLINS

Case Study #6: John's First Deal

John is a twenty year-old construction worker with a fiancée and young daughter. He got started working the system because he knew the 12 hour days he was working were not going to be enough to provide his family with the financial security he felt they deserved. In his second month working the system, he found Al, a motivated seller who was moving to Arizona to retire in the warm climate.

John found Al by calling the "For Sale" classified ads and working through the "Quick-Check" script we provided him. John discovered that Al was planning to move two months later and wanted the peace of mind knowing his property was taken care of before he left the area. Al had tried to sell the house for several months, but was unsuccessful. It seems the yellow wallpaper and dingy carpet in the otherwise pretty home turned every potential buyer off to the home.

John put together a six-year lease option on the property with a price of $141,400. This price was over $15,000 below market value for the home (already John had built a large profit into the deal for himself.)

Al had two mortgages on the property with payments of $1,200 and $300 respectively. John agreed to cover the first mortgage payment of $1,200 each month and the seller, Al, was responsible for the remaining $300 second mortgage payment.

John spent $3,000 to repaint and recarpet the house. This one simple step made it irresistible to prospective tenant-buyers. He placed his "rent to own" ad and put up several hand-made signs around the neighborhood. The signs and ads generated a lot of calls. John set up four separate showings over three weeks in order to find his tenant-buyers. In this case, it was a middle-aged couple and their teenage daughter. (See chart 9 on page 197)

John collected his first month's rent of $1,295 and an upfront option payment of $2,400. They had a two year term with a fixed purchase price of $169,984. His tenant-buyers were thrilled to be able to own this home and purchased it one year later.

John made $26,724 dollars from this one deal.

Motivated Seller		Hungry Tenant-Buyer
	$95/month	
$1200	**Rent**	$1125
	$28,584	
$141,400	**Price**	$169,984
6 Years	**Term**	1 Year
$1	**Pymt**	$2,400

Total Profits:

12 months x $95/month	+ $ 1,140
Plus spread in prices	+ $28,584
minus fix-up costs	− $ 3,000

$26,724

Chart 9

This has been a dream come true for me and my family. I always wanted more than just a job working construction but I didn't know how to get going. Then one day I went to a two-hour workshop Peter and David gave on how to buy homes in nice areas with nothing down. I don't know if it was an accident or if I was meant to be there but I am grateful that I was.

I've been in their mentorship program for less than six months and have been working the Purchase Option system part-time. Already, I know that by year's end I will make more money in real estate working part time than I make working long hours in construction.

In fact, I'm so excited about my growing real estate business I'm teaching my fiancée, Jackie, to make calls during the day to set up appointments for me to meet sellers. My goal is to do a deal a month and I know that in a year's time I'll meet it. It's like a whole new future is opening up for me and my family. I can't say enough about what Peter and David have taught me.

—John Jamison

John started out knowing nothing about investing in real estate. He had never done any investing before, but he applied himself, studied hard, and took action. The results? John has already found tenant-buyers for three different deals he has going and is looking to fill his fourth property—a ten-year lease option. If he can do it, so can *you*!

Here Is What Some of Our Other Students Are Saying About Their Experiences Investing In Real Estate Using the Purchase Option System

Dear Peter and David,

I wanted to let you know about my most recent deal. I met a home builder who hasn't been able to sell one of his houses using his normal methods. After having two offers fall through he was more than willing to accept my purchase option offer.

The neat thing is that I already had my buyer lined up for this property. All I had to do was call him and let him know that I'd found him a brand new house! As for the option money, I'll be getting $15,000 from my tenant-buyer and paying $10,000 to the home builder.

I made $5,000 by selling the house the day after I picked it up, and it should bring another $23,000 in long-term profits.

Thank you both for the help in putting this together. I'm learning that because each deal is unique, it really helps to have you guys right there with me on each one.

I remember when I first learned about your system and how scared I was to take a chance that it would work for me. My wife says to write that she appreciates the fact that you believed in me even when I had trouble believing in myself.

—JOHN SEITZ

Here's another letter from one of our beginning students, Nancy Olson:

Dear David and Peter,

I recently did my first deal and I wanted to tell you about it. I used to work as a medical assistant but had been wanting to get started in real estate for over 10 years. My biggest fear before I got started was not having enough money.

Despite these fears, I decided to move ahead, and using your system I was able to do it. I found it especially helpful to be able to call in and have my questions answered when I needed.

Total profits from this deal should be about $28,000. It used to take me two years to earn that kind of money! My advice to anyone who is hesitant to get started is to just do it! It's fun and exciting.

—Nancy Olson

Or this e-mail from one of our students in the Pacific Northwest:

Today, I can't tell you how thrilled I was as my wife and I left our first Tenant/Buyers in their new home and the balance of $5,000 Option Money and 1/2 month's rent of $720.

I found this property using the aged for rent dials. The Seller had gotten a nice promotion at work and had moved closer to the office (a 2-hour drive from this house.) She was also making double payments. She was unable to move the property with her realtor for three months.

With your methods, I came in and placed a tenant-buyer in 2 1/2 weeks. I had 164 inquiries from the 30+ signs I placed. John and Shannon were my 88th caller. So as you can see, I continued to market the property even after they left a deposit to hold it. I followed your advice to continue to market the property until my tenant buyer had paid me in full.

Here's the break down and "Locked in Profits"
* 4-year Lease with Seller
* 3-year lease with T/B
* Price to Tenant/ Buyer $209,980
* Price to Seller ($180,000)
* Security Deposit (refundable) $1,406
* Marketing Expenses ($125)
* Loan Pay Down, Estimate $3,600
* Rent Credits expected ($1,800)
* Cash Flow-three years $1,178
  ESTIMATED LOCKED IN
  PROFITS $34,239.00

Again, I just wanted to thank you and look forward to my next deal soon.

—JOHN PENA

Here is one final letter from Cindy Leavitt, one of our students in Idaho:

I am not very old, but I'm old enough to know to let people go before me and make the mistakes that I can learn from without experiencing the pain. I have already made enough money to repay the investment I made, and within the next two weeks, will be tying up a deal that will make about $27,000.00 profit…

I was one of those people that dragged my feet about investing the money because I have a "High Maintenance" family of seven and run a family-owned computer business. I felt that I could not afford to tie that money up. I finally realized I needed to take action if I wanted to begin to see profits. The only regret I have is that I didn't get started sooner.

—Cindy Leavitt

We could go on and on about the deals our students have made. But that's not really the point we are trying to make. The real point is that they were just ordinary people like you and us who grabbed onto their dreams and took action. You can do the same thing.

Heather Pederson did. Heather was in the military at the time she found her first deal: A ten -year lease-option on a 4 bedroom, 3 bath house. The seller of this property was also in the military. He had owned the home for less than a year when he was transferred to another base. He didn't have the equity in the house for him to have a real estate agent sell it unless he was willing to pay for the agent's commission out of his own pocket. Heather found a solution that met his needs and created over $30,000 of locked-in profits. If she can do this so can you. It isn't a question of whether real estate will work... the real question is, "Will you?"...

We are getting near the end of our time together. Let's shift gears a bit and talk not just about real estate, but about wealth. In the final section of this book, you are going to learn about unlimited wealth, and how you can even move beyond it!

Section Seven:

Unlimited Wealth

Everybody Can Win

There's a rumor going around that we live in a win-lose world. It rears its ugly head in many different ways. A boss and an employee argue over salary. A husband and a wife fight over how to spend the monthly income. A business struggles to drain every last cent from a customer.

The common thread of all these situations is the belief that there is only a limited amount of money in the world. This scarcity mentality says that if you make more money, then someone else must be making less money. But this just isn't so.

In reality, there is infinite wealth out there for you to create. The more service and value you give, the more wealth you generate in return.

I remember what one of our students had to say when it finally hit her that wealth was really unlimited. For most of Susan's life she had lived in fear of not having enough money. She worried over paying for her children's college education. She felt stressed over bills her family was facing. In simple terms, she constantly looked at money as if it was in short supply.

Several months after we started to work together buying properties, she and her husband came back to a training session I was conducting for some of our new mentorship students.

The change in Susan was dramatic! She was like a different person. She seemed lighter, and much happier. When I asked what the difference was, she told me that she had finally stopped worrying about money. She realized that she could create as much wealth as she wanted. And with this realization, came peace of mind.

She smiled and said, "That section of the training where Peter shifted our thinking about wealth has made a huge difference for me. I now know that there will be plenty of money available to take care of the family. It is so freeing to realize this.

—DAVID FINKEL

On the original San Diego Challenge, where I went out with three beginning students and in three days locked-up over $1.5 million worth of real estate using $37 down, I learned a lesson that was even more valuable than any of the deals we had put together.

I had just dropped off John and Margaret, two of the three students who went on the Challenge with me, at the airport terminal building. The good-byes were composed of heartfelt hugs and promises to stay in contact over time.

When I headed out to return the rental car, I realized I had lost the map that showed where I was supposed to go. I figured that I could find the place, and besides, I had plenty of time until my flight.

After driving back and forth in the area that I knew hid the rental car agency, I spotted the familiar blue and yellow sign. I pulled in, turned the keys over to the agent, and then went outside to wait for the shuttle back to the airport terminal.

As I looked out across the city skyline, I marveled at the sights and sounds. A train, with whistle blaring, blasted past to my right. Overhead, a commuter plane was coming in for its landing. I could see the blue shuttle bus coming into the parking lot. Just then, down by the street corner, I noticed a man about my height standing near a traffic light with a cardboard sign in his hands. It read, "I'm hungry. Please help."

My first reaction was an urge to reach out and help him. But almost immediately there was another thought that seeing him triggered, "He's probably just faking it. Besides, if I go over to help him, I might miss the bus and also my flight."

The first feeling grew even stronger. "Help him!"

I had learned more than ever over the last three days of the Challenge to trust in my feelings. I thought of Jesus when he said, "In as much as you did it to the least of these my brethren, you did it to me." I knew what I needed to do.

I put down my bags just as the shuttle bus was stopping in front of me. I ran as fast as I could over to this man who seemed to have been placed in my path. I reached into my pocket in search of some money to give this man. One by one I flipped through the wad of bills, each time thinking, "No, that's not enough… give more!"

Just then a goal I had written out seventeen years earlier came into my mind. At the time I was an auto mechanic making five bucks an hour. At the mall near my home I was often asked for a quarter by homeless people. I had written down the goal to have enough money to be able to give a $100 bill to someone asking for a quarter. My dreams really were coming true.

As I reached out and handed the bill to this man, my eyes locked onto his. "God bless you brother," I said. Again my feelings controlled my actions and I reached out and gave him a tremendous hug. The airplanes roaring, the sounds of the city, the waiting bus all blurred into the background.

"Pray for me," he said. I hurried back to the waiting shuttle. Just as I was stepping into the bus, I saw my new friend running up the street towards me, waving his cardboard sign to get my attention. I paused on the steps of the shuttle, oblivious to the waiting passengers. He touched his heart gently with his right hand and then stretched it out toward me.

The message was clear, "From my heart to yours, thank you." Was this God's way of thanking me for being brave enough to live my dreams? I turned and stepped into the shuttle, ignoring the grumbling of the other passengers who had to wait. I sat down and knew the Challenge had been an even greater success than I had first thought.

Once in the airport, I headed to my gate. At the security checkpoint I placed my bags on the inspection belt and turned to walk through the metal detector. There on the ground in front of me was what appeared to be the same bill I had given to my homeless friend less than twenty minutes earlier. I have never before or since found that much money in my life.

As I leaned down to pick it up, another thought flashed through my head, "Give and so it shall be given back to you."

—PETER CONTI

Truly, there is unlimited wealth out there waiting for you. The only thing you need to do is to put the strategies and techniques of this book into practice. When you apply the ideas in this book, you will be creating a massive net worth.

Imagine for a moment how good it feels to go by your

bank and know you have all the money you need to take care of yourself and your family. Think about the lives that you are now able to bless with your financial wealth. What are the expressions on their faces when they accept your gifts? What do you hear when they say "thank you?" How does all this make you feel?

Think about the freedom your money can buy. Time to spend playing with your children... Time to spend on vacation with your spouse... Time to sit and watch a sunset and feel closer to your creator...

Real estate has been a proven vehicle to create great fortunes for centuries. You already know that it is the most certain way to make money. When you are out there working as an investor helping sellers and buyers, you are creating massive value. And when you create massive value in the world, you cannot help but be compensated greatly for your efforts. How much money do you want to earn? How much value are you willing to create? Your only limit is you.

You already understand and know about all these incredible benefits of using real estate to create massive financial wealth. But there are some things that are more important than the money you make. If you want to find out what lies beyond unlimited wealth, then you'll just have to keep reading.

Beyond Unlimited Wealth

Wealth Is More Than Money

You already know that wealth is so much more than money. Wealth is your health, having a loving family, being passionate about your work, finding fulfillment in everyday life, and having total peace of mind.

The best part of the financial success you are on the road to creating is the lasting impact you'll have on those people you love most. The wealth you have is a gift to you. How you use it to bless the lives of other people is your gift back to the world.

In life, it's not the money you earn that counts—it's the lives you touch and bless that truly matter. It's not a question of what you earn, but rather what you do with what you earn.

Still, if you don't get out there and earn those dollars, you are limiting the gifts of time, freedom, and security you are able to share with yourself, your family, and your community.

Helping Other People

Right now you are probably thinking about the group of people you would like to help with your new wealth. It is a wonderful feeling to know that you are doing good in the world by giving to a worthy cause. And once you create the financial freedom you so strongly desire, you are going to have something even more important to give—your time.

You'll have the time to volunteer to help your causes. Maybe you'll use this time to visit a shut-in, or to work at a children's center, or any one of a variety of things. The point is, you will be able to spend your time in your own way and on your own terms.

We believe strongly that the only reason to have wealth is to be able to put it to good use. When we are partners with students and put a deal together, we donate ten percent of our profits to a charity we jointly choose. We have one student who supports her local battered women's shelter, another who supports Habitat for Humanity, and still another who supports programs for "at risk" children.

The remarkable thing is that we all have different groups of people we feel strongly about supporting. And when each of us takes it upon ourselves to make a difference, no matter how small, in our chosen area, everybody wins. Sharing the money-making ideas in this book is like tossing a handful of pebbles into a pond—the ripples spread wider and wider until they cover the entire area. Even though we are a small group of investors, we are able to touch thousands, even millions of lives.

When you move beyond wealth, you will enjoy so many more of life's true riches. Right now, let's just take a moment to talk through all those components you'll enjoy when you move beyond unlimited wealth.

Giving to Your Loved Ones

Have you ever felt the disappointment of not being able to give something to your family that you know they needed? Or felt the stress of worrying over meeting the family bills?

When you move beyond unlimited wealth, you'll never have to feel the uneasiness of financial limitation again.

You'll be able to provide the best of everything to your family. You'll be able to give your kids all the things you know will make a difference in their lives. You'll enjoy the inner strength and pride that comes from having the confidence that you are able to take care of those people you love most.

One of the couples we trained came to us at the beginning of our mentorship program. They shared how they desperately wanted to be able to send their kids to college but that financially they were in a bind. After they put their first three deals together, their lives were changed forever. They knew they would be able to fund their kids' college education out of the profits from the deals they were putting together in their spare time.

I'll never forget the day I met one of their sons. He shook my hand and thanked me for teaching his parents how to make money in real estate. He went on to tell me about all the exciting ideas he was learning in college. His eyes were ablaze.

As he was telling me all of this, I looked at his father standing by his side. His dad's eyes were filled with love and pride. This man and his wife were finally able to give their children the gift of a bright future. This experience has touched and inspired me to continuously find new and better ways of teaching people to create lasting wealth with real estate.

—DAVID FINKEL

Freedom

Have you ever felt pressed into a box with no way out? Stuck in a job you couldn't stand? Or locked into a schedule that took over your life?

When you move beyond unlimited wealth, you are in control of your own life. Your time is your own. You choose whom you want to see and how you want to spend your time. Never again will anyone else dictate the pace of your life. You will be the author of your own life.

How would it feel to be able to wake up each day and choose how you want to spend your time. You have no limits. Whatever you choose to do, you can do it. Where would you travel? What places have you always dreamed of seeing? Who would you visit?

When you move beyond unlimited wealth, you create the freedom to do what you want, when you want, and with whom you want.

One of the things I am most grateful for is the freedom real estate has given me. Rather than having to rush off to work each day, I am able to enjoy one of life's most precious gifts—my three-year-old son, Marston. It's early in the morning and he has just woken up. Half asleep he crawls up into my lap and I just sit there and hold him.

These moments are getting shorter and shorter as he gets older. Still, those few minutes when my son is curled up in my lap are priceless. I thank God that I am able to have the lifestyle that affords me the freedom to be there to enjoy them.

—PETER CONTI

Security

When you move beyond unlimited wealth, you are protecting yourself and your family from the financial instability that causes so much tension and anxiety in this world. You will enjoy peace of mind knowing you will always have more than enough money to take care of your needs.

Being in real estate as long as I have, I've met lots of investors who have made great fortunes only to lose them in one painful crash. That's one of the reasons I stress security so much in the Purchase Option system. It's one thing to make a few million dollars, and it's quite another to keep it.

Purchase Option investing is the safest way to create enduring wealth through real estate. Each property you own or control is kept at a distance from each new property you acquire. You will never have to leverage one property against another and then sit back and watch helplessly as one bad event sends them toppling over like dominos. Each Purchase Option technique minimizes the risk and still gives you, the investor, almost unlimited upside, profit potential.

In the end, your real security is knowing that you can live anywhere in the country and starting from scratch, build up tremendous wealth in just a few short years. Ultimately, it is your ability to create wealth that gives you that deep sense of peace and security.

—PETER CONTI

Certainty

Ask 100 random strangers if they are doing the things they know will lead them to financial freedom and 98 out of 100 will tell you no. Why not? Because on one level or another, they are afraid they can't do it. They have the fear that if they try to achieve financial success, they will fail. So they come up with elaborate stories they tell themselves or to other people. "The economy is terrible right now." "You need money to make money." "I could have made it, but…"

The real reason lying at the heart of most people's fears

is that they don't have the sense of certainty that the work they put in will be rewarded with financial success. If a person knows, with absolute certainty, that a specific plan of action will lead them to massive wealth, then they are willing to take action. It's only the lack of this proven plan that stops 98% of the population.

But you are different. You have in your hands a plan of action to succeed financially. Purchase Option real estate is your proven track to riches. When you work this plan, you know with total certainty that you will get the wealth you want.

This sense of certainty you feel in your future is the real key that moves you beyond unlimited wealth. It is the master key that unlocks the door to all the other riches awaiting you in life. Some people have called this certainty, "Faith." The name is not important. What is important is the knowledge you now have, that when you are persistent in putting the ideas from this book into action, you will achieve financial freedom. Congratulations!

Closing Thoughts

If any part of you still has any doubts or questions about how you can put this incredible system to work for you, then call our office today. Our staff will rush you some powerful information about how we can work together to create multiple streams of income buying homes in nice areas with nothing down. We are here to help you get started investing in real estate. We are here to help you turn your financial dreams into your financial reality.

In fact, when you call our office today, we'll rush you a free one hour audio cassette which shares with you exactly how you can get started buying homes in nice areas with nothing down—today! (See Appendix A)

In the end it is all up to you. You no longer have any excuses to settle for financial mediocrity. You have the knowledge for creating great wealth and now it's up to you to put these ideas and strategies into action.

It's Time for You to Make a Decision

It has been said that in times of adversity you don't have a problem to face, you have a decision to make. What is your decision going to be? Are you going to choose to give in to your fears and keep "thinking" about getting started in real estate? Or are you going to get yourself into gear and go after your dreams?

Great! We are proud that you have decided to choose the road to wealth, and the real riches that lie beyond unlimited wealth.

We wish you success on your journey, and we are here if you need us. Just give us a call.

—PETER CONTI AND DAVID FINKEL

Appendix A

"When I got started investing in real estate it felt like I was totally on my own, until one day I found..."

Free Training for Real Estate Investors!

Dear Reader,

It seems like such a short time ago I was a struggling auto mechanic.

I wish I could tell you it was easy to make my first million. It wasn't (although the second million was a lot easier.)

For those of you who have just finished this book it might seem like I had it easy when I got started investing in real estate, but I didn't.

When I got started, I was scared of doing it all by myself and I was overwhelmed not knowing where to begin. I learned the slow, hard way, by making mistakes and paying the price.

That's why when the American Real Estate Investors Association (AREIA) asked me to sponsor this year's membership drive, I was thrilled.

You see, AREIA was the association I wished I had way back when I got started.

217

The American Real Estate Investors Association (AREIA) is a nationwide group of real estate investors who have joined together to help each other be more successful investors.

The association not only gives you the chance to network with other success-minded investors, but it also provides you with ongoing support and training.

The bottom line is that AREIA helps its members make more money with less work, risk, and effort.

Do You Know The One Secret All Successful Real Estate Investors Have In Common?

Napoleon Hill in his breakthrough best-selling book, Think and Grow Rich (the granddaddy of all self-help non-fiction books) described the one thing every one of the 500 most successful people had in common.

This is the same secret all of today's real estate millionaires and billionaires still have in common. And this commonly overlooked little-known idea is the most important reason for you to join AREIA.

This secret is something Napoleon Hill called having a "mastermind group." A mastermind group is a group of two or more people joining together in a spirit of mutual harmony, trust, and respect, for the attainment of a definite chief aim in a way that every member benefits on an ongoing basis.

AREIA is the mastermind group of investors across the country for you to "get together" with regularly to help you and the other members be more successful as real estate investors.

"If only I didn't have to go to work today..."

Have you ever felt like you were stuck in a dead end job. Or maybe you're comfortable, too comfortable, and you would like to break out and take control of your financial future.

All our members have dealt with this at one point. Many of them slowly worked themselves out of the rat race and into real estate full time over the course of 3 to 5 years. Others took the leap of faith and did it in 12 months or less.

And other members simply invest part time, continuing to work a full time job. They work the job to pay their bills and they invest in real estate to create a huge nest egg for retirement.

The Three Biggest Reasons Our Members Joined (And why you should too!)

Reason #1: They were tired of doing it all alone.

Can you relate to this one? You are out there doing your best to buy and sell properties and make money. But it feels like you're totally on your own.

By joining AREIA you don't have to be hanging in the wind, doing all your investing with no one to bounce ideas off of, no one to turn to for questions, to brag to, or simply to complain a little bit to about what a hard time you had on a specific deal.

Our members are all in the same boat and you have the opportunity to network with them through the member discussion area of our Web site, through our regular conference calls, through the voice mail system, and at our regional and national investment superconferences.

This is one of the biggest reasons many of our members joined—to have a network of other success-minded investors they can turn to for support and input.

Our members know that together they can accomplish far more than by doing it all alone.

Reason #2: They wanted access to the ongoing training.

To make big money in real estate requires specialized knowledge.

Part of AREIA's mission is to provide you with ongoing training and education to help you be more successful in your investing.

One of the biggest benefits of membership is free access to the members only section of our Web site with tons of powerful ideas to help you with your investing.

You'll also get access to our interactive voice mail system with its dozens of archived audio training-on-demand classes and linked focus groups.

You'll get access to our newsletter and special tele-conference classes.

And you'll get access to regional training conferences held throughout the year, all over the country.

AREIA will bring the nation's top real estate experts to you, all through the wonders of technology.

Reason #3: They wanted help knowing exactly how to get started investing.

Probably the single biggest reason most of our members joined initially was because they wanted help knowing where to begin.

Starting off investing in real estate can sure feel scary. All the choices and decisions you have to make by yourself can seem overwhelming.

AREIA has helped its new members know exactly what they need to do to make money investing in real estate. There is a profound truth in the statement that successful people are willing to share their success with other like-minded people.

Because many of our members have multi-million dollar portfolios and have created success for themselves as investors, they get great pleasure helping out new investors.

By joining AREIA, you'll be able to post questions onto our private Web site or through the interactive voice mail system and get answers from people who have done it themselves.

This real world advice will help you reach your goals and dreams faster than you ever thought possible.

"What if I'm Already A Member of a Local Real Estate Investment Group?"

Most of our members are also members of their local investor group. Let's face it, there is something powerful about being involved with your local investor group. If you are fortunate enough to be in an area with a local real estate investment group, I urge you to visit the meetings and consider joining.

Our members simply use AREIA as another tool to make them even more successful in their investing.

They like the timely information and ongoing training that comes from being a part of a nationwide network of investors.

They tell us that the best part of all is that they can tap into 90% of this insider information from their own homes through their phones, faxes, e-mails, and internet connections. They love the convenience and speed at which they learn, network, and grow as investors.

Here's what some of our members have to say about how AREIA has helped them take their investing business to the next level:

"After I bought my second investment property I got scared. It felt like I was out there all alone. I really get a lot out of the support that comes from being part of a nationwide investor network."
—CHERYL HASTINGS, SALEM, OREGON

"The other day I heard a message that was broadcast on the voice mail system that helped me avoid a HUGE mistake on a deal I was working on. I have come to rely on the voice mail system to keep me out of trouble and making smart decisions."
—MARTIN KIND, BALTIMORE, MARYLAND

Now we get to the heart of this letter...

When AREIA came to me to head up their Annual Membership Drive, we sat down and talked about the best ways to dramatically increase membership. When all was said and done we realized that there was only one way to get this done...

Let you join risk-free and try out what being a member is like for yourself. That's why...

Now you can try out being a member of the American Real Estate Investors Association risk-free for an entire year!

And if at any point within the year you are not totally thrilled and satisfied, simply let AREIA know and you will get a complete, no questions asked, refund of your ENTIRE annual membership fee.

This means you can try out being a member. When you feel you are getting great value, you'll continue your membership, taking advantage of all the benefits. And if you aren't satisfied for any reason, you take us up on this UNCONDITIONAL guarantee. Either way you win. You have nothing to lose, but so much to gain!

And here are two final perks of joining right now that will make this offer irresistible to any investor who is serious about making money:

Take us up on this limited offer and you will also get the following bonuses absolutely free. And even if you decide to cancel your membership later on, you still get to keep both bonuses as our gift to you.

Bonus #1: A FREE 90 minute video! Watch as Peter Conti teaches a live workshop on using the Purchase Option System to make money investing in real estate.(Value: $69)

Bonus #2: A $100 certificate valid towards the AREIA Annual Investor Super Conference! This means you'll save a hundred bucks when you come to this 2-day intensive workshop held each January. (Value: $100)

And remember, even if you do decide to cancel later, you keep both bonuses as our gift.

The annual membership fee is so ridiculously low that I'm almost embarrassed to tell you. Just remember, AREIA is an investor association, not a big business. (When you join we hope you'll eventually choose to get involved and maybe even volunteer on one of the committees.)

Your annual membership fee is simply $69.

To join, just have a credit card handy and call our automated toll-free membership hotline at 800-695-9512 ext. 850 (you can call 24 hours a day, 7 days a week.)

Thank you for taking the time to listen to me and I hope you decide to try out this risk-free trial offer.

Remember, working together we can all achieve so much more, so join today. You can join on-line at www.americanreia.com. Or for the fastest, easiest way to join, simply call 800-695-9512 ext. 850.

All my best,

Peter

P.S. Remember that if at any point over the entire year you aren't fully satisfied with your membership, just contact AREIA and you'll get a prompt, courteous, no questions asked refund. And you'll get to keep the $169 of BONUSES as our gift!

P.S. You can also join online at www.americanreia.com.

12 MONTH SUBSCRIPTION TO

The Purchase Option Investor's Newsletter

This free newsletter is filled with inside tips and techniques to help you make money using the Purchase Option strategies you've just finished learning about.
Your issue will be e-mailed to you at the beginning of each month.

Sign Up At: www.resultsnow.com

or
Fax This Form to: 877-626-8673

Name_____

Address_____

City_____State_____Zip_____

Phone(   )_____

E-mail_____@_____

Appendix B: Success Library

Learning Resources Available to Help You Succeed Buying Homes In Nice Areas With Nothing Down

Street Smart Marketing Secrets: How to Find Motivated Sellers, Hungry Buyers and Eager Renters

Have you ever wondered what it would be like to have motivated sellers calling you—begging you to buy their property? Wouldn't it be nice to have scores of hungry buyers and eager renters competing for your homes and apartments— driving prices and rents through the roof? Here's your chance to learn how to have all this and much more. It's all part of the **Street Smart Marketing Secrets** course.

Here's your chance to pick the brain of two of America's top real estate experts. With your course you'll get the video tape, **"Insider Marketing Secrets: Maximum Profits—Minimum Effort"** and two audio tapes, **"5 Fun, Easy Ways to Find Hungry Buyers and Eager Renters"** and **"Still More Ways to Find Motivated Sellers."**

In this powerful real estate investment course you'll learn:
- **27** powerful techniques for finding motivated sellers!
- How to create **multiple streams of income** by renting your properties for top dollar!
- A simple three-step formula to <u>whet the appetite of buyers</u> and renters to get them to *act now*!

- <u>Four magic words</u> that can **triple** your ad response!
- The **8** *hottest* benefits you can offer a motivated seller to get him to call you immediately!
- The 6 ways to **cash in** on your real estate contacts—*instantly*!
- The 12-step system to find a buyer or renter for your property **today**!
- How to turn your biggest competitor into your best source of leads.
- A <u>little-known secret</u> to increase your ability to find motivated sellers by up to **500%**!!!
- Your four biggest guns to fill your properties fast (and how you must use them!)
- *Money-saving* AND *money-making* guerrilla marketing tactics you can use to take your real estate business to the next level!

Plus, as a reward for reading this book you'll get the following three free bonus items:

Bonus #1 40-Page Special Report that reveals:

- How to set up money-making relationships with realtors —with five ways to turn these relationships into **paydays** for you!
- **The biggest mistake** most investors make (and three specific strategies for you to avoid it)!
- How to get buyers to call you *begging* to buy your house (And what to say to them when they do call)!
- How to create a ready reserve of buyers and renters so that on future deals, you make your money faster and with **less effort!**

Bonus #2: 11 professionally written and designed, camera ready marketing pieces:

- Two business card layouts
- Two flyers to get motivated sellers to call you
- Two flyers to attract hungry renters and buyers
- Four voice mail scripts to use with both motivated sellers and renters/buyers (Written by one of the nation's top copywriting experts and proven to work in the only place that counts—the real world!)

Bonus #3: The exact classified ad that helped a small group of investors on the original San Diego Challenge lock-up over $1.5 million worth of real estate in only three days — with only $37 down!!!

Catalog Number: 004 Street Smarts Marketing Secrets Course

Your Investment: $39.97
(Including all three bonus items)

To Order See Success Library Order Form On Page 277
Or Call 1-800-952-9585 ext. 825

The Inner Secrets
Quick-Start Action Pack!

This past December 8-10, Peter Conti and David Finkel led a band of three beginning investors to San Diego, California to make good on their challenge to the press. Not only did they meet their goal of $250,000 for each student—**they doubled it!** <u>That's right, they locked up over $1.5 million worth of real estate—ten separate properties—with only $37 down!</u>

Here's your chance to learn exactly how they did it—and how you can too!!! Right now, you have the special opportunity to order the **Quick-Start Action Pack**. With your action pack, you'll get the two audio cassettes: *How to Buy Homes In Nice Areas With Nothing Down! and How to Find Motivated Sellers From the Comfort of Your Home.*

You'll also get a 71 page, detailed manual bursting with hidden shortcuts and insider investment secrets that took them years to learn (and are guaranteed to make you thousands of dollars!)

In this intensive course, you'll learn the most powerful nothing down strategy in existence. And you'll learn the specific techniques to put this strategy to work for you—creating "hands off" residual streams of income for you!

You'll learn:
* Five Fun, Easy Ways to Earn Up to an **Extra $100,000 This Year** Investing in Real Estate!

230

- How to Enjoy All the Benefits of Owning Property without Any of the Risks or Hassles!
- Wealth Without Risk: How to Build a Million Dollar Net Worth in Three Years or Less—<u>Working From Home!</u>
- How to Use **Lease-Options** in a New Way to Make More Money With *Less* Effort!

Plus, as a reward for reading this book, you'll get the following three *free* bonus items:

Bonus #1: Free Video!

The 12 Keys to Negotiate Your Way to Anything You Want

- How to avoid the biggest mistake most negotiators make (it's costing you thousands on every deal!)
- **A little-known** technique to get the other side to mention all the numbers first—every time!
- The key to understanding how much power you actually have in a negotiation! (and much, much more!)

Bonus #2: Free Audio Tape!

21 Powerful Secrets for Finding Motivated Sellers

- How to create money-making relationships with real estate professionals (so they send you deal after deal!)
- Over 21 different ways for you to find motivated sellers! (and what to ask them when you do find them!)

231

3 Free Tele-Training Sessions - Order now and you'll also get to attend these three intensive 60 minute classes from your home over the telephone!

You'll learn:
- How to buy your first (or next) investment property in 90 days or less!
- How a newlywed made over $22,000 in locked-in profits on her very first deal (and how you can too!)
- How a retired minister made over $19,000 in locked-in profits on his very first deal (and how you can too!)

This is your chance to pick the brain of one of the nation's top real estate experts! You'll learn the inside secrets and real world strategies you need to take your real estate investment success to the next level and how to put the Inner Secrets Action Pack to work making you money!

Catalog Number: 008 Quick-Start Action Pack

Your Investment: $99 (Including all three bonus items)

To Order See Success Library Order Form On Page 277
Call 1-800-952-9585 ext. 825

The Seven MasterSkills Of Highly Successful Investors

For the past seven years, our students have turned to us with their toughest questions and their greatest successes...

Now for the first time ever — You can learn how our top students are closing one to four deals a month—and how you can too!

Why is it some investors can consistently close four deals a month while other investors struggle to find their first deal?

Over the past seven years, we've worked with thousands of investors — seasoned experts and beginners — and we've made a **startling discovery**: The successful investors all had developed seven core skills and honed these skill to a fine edge. The investors who had mastered these skills were buying millions of dollars worth of real estate and enjoying doing it!

In this detailed home study course, you'll learn all seven MasterSkills so that you can make more money with less effort.

How would you like to have this same sense of unshakable confidence these top performers have? Here's your chance!

Getting You These Breakthrough Ideas
The Quickest, Easiest Way Possible

We knew we had to find a way to share these amazing findings with you in a concentrated and systematized format. This breakthrough new home study course, called *The Seven MasterSkills of Highly Successful Investors,* is designed to help you **master ALL seven** skills so you have a clear road map towards financial freedom.

Here Are the Seven MasterSkills
Of Highly Successful Investors

Master Skill One:Negotiating

Without exception, all of our most successful students have honed their ability to negotiate money-making win-win agreements to a razor's edge.

Have you ever left a negotiation with a seller uneasy, thinking you should have done better for yourself? In this section, you'll learn how you can make sure that never happens again!

You'll learn:
* How to make negotiating fun and easy!
* How to negotiate with out-of-state owners so they agree to your terms over the phone and Fed Ex their signed and notarized contracts back within 72 hours!
* How to renegotiate with a seller to tweak the deal so it fits their needs better and makes you even more money!
* The most costly mistake you can make while negotiating AND how you can avoid it!

234

- Nine techniques to help you put together the best deal possible!
- A little-known sentence that will make you up to five thousand dollars every time you use it!

You'll also learn how one of our students consistently gets a seller to drop his price and give him a longer term—all by asking two simple questions up-front. This one secret alone is worth thousands of dollars to you—this year!

Another technique you'll be learning was used by two of our students to renegotiate and close their first deals.

One student used it to get the seller to drop his price by over **$8,300** <u>with just one phone call!</u> **You'll learn how!**

The other student used this secret to turn his three-year lease option term into a **six** year term <u>in less than two minutes time!</u> **You'll learn how to do the exact same thing!**

MasterSkill Two: Handling Questions and Objections

Our successful students have all mastered the answers to the <u>five most common objections from sellers.</u> **In this section, you'll get these answers scripted word for word. This means that you'll have the same success these other winning investors are already enjoying.**

You'll learn how to handle objections like:
"I don't want to lease my property, I just want to sell it!"

"I won't go for such a long term."
"I need to run this past my attorney."

You'll learn how NOT to tell the seller too much on the phone and exactly how to use each question he asks as an opportunity to move closer to a *money-making deal.* Imagine the confidence you'll feel knowing that you can handle anything he throws at you.

Plus!!! You'll also learn how to handle the three most common objections of tenant-buyers and how to frame each objection as a huge benefit to them. This will get them to nod their heads, saying "yes" to your deal and leave them smiling.

MasterSkill Three:
Leveraging Your Time and Efforts to Produce More Results With Less Energy

Successful investors know that the most critical element of their success is how they fit their investing in with the other parts of their lives. They know that time is their most precious resource and that they must maximize its use.

In this mind-expanding section, you'll learn how to avoid the three biggest time-wasters that snare most investors and how to make every action you take more effective.

You'll learn:
• How to get other people to go out and find you deals!
• The one question you must ask before you meet with a seller or you are wasting your time!

- A little-known secret to help you triple your results finding motivated sellers
- How to get other people to sort through the classified ads for you and give you only the best leads (This one idea will free up hours of your time EVERY week! And it's so simple!)
- How you can create a mastermind network of advisors to help you put together winning deals

This one section alone will be worth many times more than your investment in this home study course. When you're done with this section, your investing business will be *streamlined and highly* focused. **You'll find that all your efforts are producing bigger and bigger results... with less effort!**

This means that while all your competitors are out there wasting time and energy with ineffective strategies, you'll be several steps ahead of them. <u>You'll be closing more deals and making more money</u>.

MasterSkill Four:
Finding Deals No One Else Knows About

Real estate isn't so much about property as it is about people. Because of this, you need to be able to tap into an ever-flowing stream of sellers and buyers for you to make it big in real estate.

<u>We've watched students of ours consistently find several deals each and every month—working part time— in every type of real estate market</u>.

It never ceases to amaze us how two of our students in

the same city can have such dramatically different results. One student will call us and say he can't find any deals. And a few minutes later another of our students in the same city will call us up and ask for our help in putting together his **fourth deal that month!**

What causes these different results? It's simple. Some of our students have made it a point to <u>master how to find</u> <u>consistent sources of motivated sellers and hungry buyers</u> <u>other investors don't know about.</u>

In this section, you are going to learn the essential skill of creating a steady stream of new deals flowing into your real estate business. In fact, after studying this section, you'll have so many new ways of finding motivated sellers that you might just be calling us up (like one of our students did recently) and asking us if it is possible to be doing too many deals at once! (Now isn't that a problem you'd love to have!)

MasterSkill Five:
Developing the Confidence and Knowledge To
Evaluate the Risks and Rewards of
New Deals—Fast!

Have you ever met with a seller and wondered if you should be buying their house or not? There you are, the seller is ready to sign the deal, and you are wondering if it is a sound decision to do the deal.

After learning from this intensive section, you'll never be left wondering that again. You're going to learn the four criteria of all good deals. And, more importantly, you are going to master the skill of measuring all new deals up to these four critical criteria and making only smart choices.

MasterSkill Six:
Maximizing Your Profits From Your Properties by Increasing Your Up-Front Income, Monthly Streams of Cash-flow, and Long Term Profit

One of the biggest differences we have observed between the most successful investors and those who struggle is what they do with properties after they buy or take control of them.

The average investor struggles to find an end user for the property, and as a direct result of this, he is often put into a tough financial position. This forces him to sell or lease the property from a motivated position and this spells trouble with a capital "T" for him.

In this section you'll learn:

How you can turn your properties into hands-off, passive investments that create monthly streams of income for you.

A little-known question to ask your buyer to get them to put up to 50% more money down on your property. Three steps you need to take to qualify potential buyers on the phone to save you time and money.

The one criteria that MUST be met before you ever pass over control of your property to someone else. (If you don't follow this critical rule then you're flirting with disaster. We know! We've learned this one the hard way!) Learn from our experiences and make sure you safely and intelligently transform your investments into multiple streams of passive income.

MasterSkill Seven:
Learning and Mastering New Investment Strategies and Skills on an Ongoing Basis

The most successful investors we know NEVER stop investing in their own capacity to make money. This means that they are constantly reading books, listening to tapes, attending seminars, and working with mentors to increase their knowledge of how to make money in real estate.

Experience is the only way you'll ever learn. It's only a question of whether or not it will be your experience or someone else's.

<u>Now, for the first time ever, you'll hear about our five biggest investment mistakes, and how you can avoid ever making them yourself.</u> **All totaled these mistakes put close to $1,000,000.00 of our money at risk!**

In the past, we have never shared these costly mistakes — they're not fun to think about. But we know that our experiences can save you from making these same painful mistakes. So we've decided to tell it like it is, letting you learn from our blunders, and saving you thousands of dollars and a tremendous amount of stress and worry.

Are you committed to taking your real estate investing to the next level of success?

This is your chance to do it. Imagine analyzing and modeling how our top students have become tremendously successful and how you can too. We've compressed years of other people's experience into this intensive home study course so that you'll have the concrete tools and strategies you need to make money investing in real estate.

Your Course Comes COMPLETE With:
Twelve (12) Audio Cassettes
200+ page manual
Phone Scripts and Sample Marketing Materials

Catalog Number: 007 The Seven MasterSkills of Highly Successful Investors
Your Investment: $297

To Order See Success Library Order Form On Page 277
Or Call 1-800-952-9585 ext. 825

The Protégé Program

For the First Time Ever, the Entire Purchase Option System Is Available In a Powerful New Home Study System Called the Protégé Program!

What if you knew how to buy millions of dollars of property with nothing down? How much would this be worth to you?

For the first time ever, you can test our break-through real estate system to prove that it works… You're the judge! I'll even give you $1,100 worth of bonuses as an "ethical bribe" to encourage you to go for it (more on this later…) You either end up using the system to make you a big pile of money or you get to keep all $1,100 in free bonuses as my gift to you! Either way you win big time!

Learn How to Buy Homes In Nice Areas With Nothing Down!

It's called Purchase Option investing. This powerful new system harnesses the old ways of making money with real estate like "lease-options" and "owner carry financing" and transforms them into a breakthrough new system where your profits are multiplied and your efforts are leveraged.

Whether you're a first time investor who needs to learn from the ground up or you're an experienced hand simply looking for a few more ideas to supercharge your investing, the Purchase Option system is exactly what you need to take your investing to the next level.

242

You don't need thousands of dollars or perfect credit either! This system will teach you to start where you are and with what you have, and in 90 days or less you can be on the road to wealth.

This system not only gives you the big picture, but more importantly, it reveals the critical details that let you put all of this money-making knowledge into use creating the life of your dreams.

Here's what just a few other investors have to say about the program:

"Using the ideas and contracts you covered in your system, I did five deals during my first 18 months investing and made over $100,000 in locked in profits! Your system is great and I highly recommend it."
—JOHN JAMISON, CA

"You made it all very simple for me to understand and apply. I've picked up 15 houses now and have turned a part-time business into huge nest egg for retirement. Please feel free to tell anyone who is thinking about getting any of your materials that I think they were the best money I ever spent (considering I've made over $250,000 in locked in profits back, that is quite an understatement!)"
—CHERYL HASTINGS, OR

"I am a full-time real estate investor and I've been doing in-home selling for 20+ years. I thought I was effective, but the "Instant Offer System" is way beyond what I was doing. It has probably doubled if not tripled my success rate."
—FRANK SMOOT, MD

"We have just about every investing course out there in our library and your four courses are among the best. On just the first two deals we did after getting your system, we made over $75,000. We especially like your cutting-edge approach to negotiating. No one else out there has your finesse in scripting presentations and handling objections."
—Mark Fissore & Trish Talbot, CA

"Since I had no background in real estate investing, it was truly a dream come true for me to be able to buy my first investment home at 35% below market value with no money down...Your simple step-by-step instructions allowed me to do it. I highly recommend your system to other investors. I'm thrilled with the value."
—Neil Vermillion, OH

"My tenant buyer is about to close on the house from my first Purchase Option deal... my net is $85,000... Please feel free to use me as a reference for your programs any time, in any way, shape, or form you deem helpful."
—Mark Hardcastle, CO

"I've tried all the well-known real estate courses. I feel I wasted a lot of time and money with the others. Your course is very down to earth, practical, and provides realistic, profitable objectives that anyone can achieve. I signed my first deal using the techniques taught. The first deal provided $5,000 up front money and $34,000 in locked in profits on a three-year lease purchase. What a great feeling it was when my wife and I left our tenant-buyers in their new home. I highly recommend this system."
—John Pena, WA

"I only invest part-time. I use it to fund my other passions. Using your system, I was able to net over $100,000 in my first three years investing. Not bad, considering I only worked an average of 7-10 hours per week!"
—WILL LIMON, CO

The system includes over 1,050 pages of money-making ideas in five separate manuals along with 36 hours of audio workshops! (Later you'll see a detailed list of exactly what you'll get with your home study course.)

But first, let's take a quick tour of exactly what you'll learn from this breakthrough home study system that is divided into five separate sections...

Part I:
How to Create Multiple Streams of Income Buying Homes In Nice Areas With Nothing Down

This is the comprehensive system overview. In this concentrated section, you'll learn how to find, structure, and close money-making Purchase Option deals.

You'll learn:
* The most powerful nothing-down strategies in existence!
* How to create growing streams of monthly cash-flow from your properties!
* The four pitfalls to traditional investing and how you can safely sidestep them!

245

- Five fun, easy ways to earn up to an extra $100,000 this year investing in real estate!
- The simplest source of instant funding for your properties!
- How to turn deals into quick-cash—In 60 days or less!
- How to get "financing" for your properties without ever having to talk with a banker!
- How to set up your deals so that you increase your up-front profits, create monthly streams of cash-flow, and build in big "back-end" profits!
- Seven ways you get paid from Purchase Option deals (and why most investors overlook two of them, leaving thousands of dollars on the table.)
- The real secret of nothing down deals
- How to sidestep the landlord trap
- How to create multiple streams of income
- The seven most common mistakes investors make (and how to avoid them)
- 17 Case studies to help you see exactly how to structure money-making Purchase Option deals
- And much more...

Part II:
How to Find Motivated Sellers

The critical key to unlocking hundreds of thousands of dollars from real estate is finding a "motivated seller."

When you find a motivated seller, not only will you make a lot of money, but more importantly you will feel good about being able to help solve his problems. In all, you'll learn 63 different ways to find motivated sellers!

You'll Learn:

- The five fastest ways to find your first deal!
- The one question you MUST ask sellers before you ever meet with them—or you're wasting your time!
- How to create a steady stream of new deals flowing into your real estate business!
- How to turn your biggest competitor into one of your best sources of new deals!
- How to find landlords who are desperate to sell you their rental property for nothing down!
- Nine little-known sources for finding motivated sellers and how you can tap into each one of them!
- How to set up money-making relationships with Realtors—and five ways to turn these relationships into paydays for you!
- The single biggest mistake you can make when talking with a Realtor (and how to avoid it!)
- 15 ways to get other people to bring you profitable deals!
- How to leverage your time to find more deals faster!
- How to get sellers to call you—begging you to buy their property!
- The four magic words that can double the response to all your marketing materials!
- A simple 3-step formula to leverage your time and money finding motivated sellers
- How to make big money in a small town investing in real estate!
- A secret source of motivated sellers that is overlooked by 99% of all investors
- How to consistently find deal after deal in any city— no matter what the market is like!
- The cheapest way to get sellers to call you!

247

- Three little-known secrets for finding deals in a smaller market!
- This is your chance to learn by following a proven system for finding motivated sellers.

Just this section alone comes with 27 camera-ready and sample marketing pieces. It also includes 15 copyrighted scripts to use with sellers. In all, you'll learn dozens of proven techniques for finding deals.

Section III:
The Instant Offer System—How to Get Sellers to Say "YES!" to Your Creative Offer

Once you have found your motivated seller, it's time to sit down with him to figure out how you can help him AND make a profit. You'll learn to solve his problems in a way that leaves the seller feeling good about the deal and makes you a healthy profit.

You'll learn the specific questions you need to ask to "diagnose" the seller's real needs... and how to word your offer to get the seller to say "yes" to the deal.

This section of the system includes an in-depth manual with our copyrighted forms and contracts. These are the exact same contracts we use in our own investing. We've invested thousands of dollars to get them just right and they are yours—FREE—as part of the program.

248

You'll even get them on CD-ROM so you can just fill in the blanks and print out professional contracts at the push of a button!

Here is just a PARTIAL list of all the forms and contracts that you'll get:

- Property Escrow Document Checklist
- Escrow Instructions
- Residential Lease Purchase Agreement
- Memorandum of Option
- Additionally Insured Agreement
- Authorization for Direct Payment
- Authorization for Release of Information
- Agreement for the Purchase of Real Estate (Buying)
- Agreement to Sell Real Estate (Buying Subject to)
- Deposit to Hold the Property Form
- Tenant Buyer Lease Agreement
- Tenant Buyer Option Agreement
- Rental Applications (one and three page versions)
- Performance Deed of Trust
- Assignment of Contract Agreement
- Purchase Agreement (Selling)
- "As Is" Purchase Agreement (Selling)
- Tenant Buyer Pricing Worksheet
- Lead Based Paint Disclosure Form and Report
- Earnest Money Promissory Note
- And much more!

Plus You'll Learn:
- The most powerful question you can ask a seller to determine his real needs!
- Nine techniques to put together the best deal possible!

- A simple technique to guarantee you a quick decision from the seller (this one idea alone will save you days of frustration and wasted effort!)
- The single biggest mistake you can make when negotiating (and how you can avoid it!)
- How to get any seller to instantly drop his price just by asking two simple questions!
- How to get the seller to ask you for a lease-purchase term of five to seven years!
- The four steps you need to take to get the seller to sign the deal now!
- How to create intense desire on the other side to put together a winning deal!
- A five-step formula that will help you close the deal—time after time!
- How to get the seller to agree to all the numbers of your offer BEFORE you ever present it!
- 21 little-known factors to close Purchase Option deals
- How to word your creative offer so the seller finds it irresistible!
- Five deal killers and how to keep them from stealing your profits!
- The three key clauses you need to use to lower your risk to the absolute minimum!
- A little-known phrase to add to your paperwork that will earn you up to an extra $25,000 on every deal you do! (This one technique alone is worth 10 times the investment in this system to you!)
- Three Keys to wording your offer
- Eight questions to ask the seller that uncover his real reasons for selling
- How to handle the five biggest seller objections (including a scripted response to the "attorney objection")

- Nine (9) Negotiating pitfalls that can kill your deal (and how you can safely sidestep them)
- Blank by blank how to fill out your contracts
- How to walk the seller through the contract and still get them to sign on the spot
- Three ways to lock in your profits on your Purchase Option deals

Part IV
How to Find Tenant Buyers

Congratulations on getting the property signed up. Now it's time for you to finish the last step of any Purchase Option deal: finding your "tenant-buyer."

You'll learn exactly how to find and sign up your tenant-buyers in the fastest, simplest, most systematic way. You'll also get all the contracts and forms you need to take care of the paperwork to protect your interests.

You'll Learn:
- A 12-step game plan for filling your property fast!
- How to determine how much rent to charge (and why this one fact is so critical to your success!)
- How you can structure the deal with your tenant-buyer so that you enjoy monthly cash-flow and huge back-end profits!
- The biggest mistake you can make when looking for your tenant-buyer—And how you can easily avoid ever making it!
- The nine critical areas of your properties that must show well (or your prospective buyer will walk!)
- 29 point tenant-buyer Checklist

- A little-known secret for renting any property in any area within 72 hours or less!
- How to get top rent and price for your property!
- The single biggest factor in getting your buyer to say "YES!"
- 12 steps to reel in your tenant-buyer when you have him on the hook
- How to create intense competition for your properties—driving the price and your profits up!
- The single biggest time-waster in marketing your property and how to avoid it!
- How to "program" potential buyers to say "yes" to the property BEFORE they ever see it!
- Exactly what to say to potential buyers when you meet them at the property!
- How to get the buyer to give you more money up-front and pay higher than market rent!
- The single cheapest way to advertise your property!
- A simple, three-step formula for whetting the appetites of buyers so they act now!
- The five most common mistakes investors make when conducting rent surveys
- A little-known technique for getting buyers to qualify themselves for you without you ever having to talk with them personally!
- How to fill out the proper paperwork to make sure you have maximum protection and minimum risk.
- Three ways your tenant-buyer can build equity before ever "owning" the property
- Our single best ad to get tons of prospective tenant-buyers calling you now
- Four steps to create tremendous curb appeal

- The five most common mistakes investors make when looking at comparables (and how to get comparables for free!)
- What to do if your tenant-buyer stops paying you rent
- Two simple steps to make sure your seller doesn't get cold feet
- How to cancel your agreement with the seller if you don't find your tenant-buyer (including two sample deal cancellation letters)
- 17 Ways you can offset negative cashflow

Part V
The 90 Day Quick-Start Action Plan

The final portion of the system is the 90 Day Quick-Start Action Plan.

This step-by-step plan of action gives you the proven steps you need to take—today—to put all this money-making information into action. Included are all the forms and information you need to keep yourself on track.

These ideas have worked for thousands of other investors and now it's your turn!

No matter what your real estate background, the Protégé Program will give you concrete tools to make more money investing in real estate and will lay out a step-by-step system for you to do it the simplest way possible.

Try out this break-through real estate system to prove that it works... You be the judge! You either end up using the system to make tens of thousands of dollars on deal after deal, or simply send it back within 90 days for a prompt, courteous, refund.

That's right, you get a 100% money-back guarantee for a full 90 days!

This gives you a full three months to "test-drive" the entire Purchase Option system, and if it doesn't meet your exacting standards, send it back (I know you won't want to part with it) and keep all $1,100 of these free bonuses as my gift to you for your efforts. Act now and you'll get these two valuable bonuses:

Bonus #1: Three Investor Tele-Classes

Learn from some of the nation's top real estate trainers right over the phone! Each class is a full hour of the latest investing ideas and techniques designed to help you get going with your investing right away! You'll be able to listen to the answers you need during each Tele Class. This is the ideal complement to get you up to speed as fast as possible with the Protégé System. ($100 value)

Bonus #2: Free Deal Consultation

And when you call to order your Protégé Program right now, you'll also get a $1,000 deal consultation from us and our staff—absolutely FREE!!!

That's right! You'll get a certificate that entitles you to a $1,000 deal consultation. This means the next time you are working a deal and need our expertise and guidance, our staff will personally spend up to an hour on the phone with you helping you structure and close the deal! This one bonus alone is worth your entire investment for the program!

And you'll get these $1,100 worth of bonuses— FREE—just for trying out the system! That makes this offer better than risk-free!

Even if you decide to return the program, keep both bonuses as our gift to you for giving both the Protégé Program and yourself a good faith effort!

You can only win! Either you love the program and use it to make tens of thousands of dollars… or it doesn't cost you a cent AND you get $1,100 in bonuses—absolutely free!

We've taken all the risk of trying out the program and put it squarely onto our shoulders.

Why? Because we know the program is that good. It's worked for so many other investors, of all experience levels, that we know it will work for you too. You have nothing to lose and so much to gain. Order Now!

This course comes COMPLETE with:
* Five (5) Comprehensive Manuals (over 1050 pages)
* 36 Audio CD's
* 44 Forms and Contracts
* 45 Sample and Camera-Ready Marketing Pieces
* 16 Sample Phone and Voice Mail Scripts
* CD-ROM of Essential Contracts (In Both Text and
* Microsoft Word Formats)
* Free Three Session Tele Class
* One Free Deal Consultation

Catalog Number: 009 The Protégé Program
Your Investment: $1297

"Would You Like to Buy Properties, No Matter What Your Credit Is Like, Without Ever Having to Talk to a Banker?"

How to Find, Close, And Sell Properties Using the Existing Financing

In this advanced home-study course, you'll learn exactly how to tap into the money-making power and security of buying properties "subject to" the existing financing.

What this means to you is:
You <u>Own</u> the Property!
You Get <u>All</u> the Tax Benefits!
You Get <u>All</u> the Appreciation!
You Get <u>All</u> the Equity Pay Down!
You Get <u>All</u> the Cash-flow!
<u>(*BUT* you never had to talk with a bank, you never had to personally guarantee a loan, you never had to qualify for the mortgage!)</u>

There are no banks to qualify with, closing paperwork is streamlined and straightforward, and you maintain iron-grip control over the properties you buy.

If terms like "All Inclusive Trust Deed," "Wrap-around Mortgage," and "Subject to Financing" sound like Greek to you, then you need this course because without it you're missing out on thousands of dollars of simple, easy profits.

You'll Learn:

- Step-by-step how to simply *take over* someone's payments and property in the safest, simplest way possible!
- The three landmines that can kill your deals and how to safely sidestep them!
- How to find sellers who are literally willing to "give" you their properties
- How to neutralize the five biggest dangers of these types of deals
- How you can close fast (even in 48 hours if needed!)
- How to stay in control of the deal at all times
- How to avoid the legal traps of "subject to" deals
- How to increase your cash-flow and make an extra $25,000 when you re-sell the property
- Five keys to getting sellers to call you, begging you to buy their property
- How to avoid the eight pitfalls of "subject to" deals
- How to use corporations and land trusts to avoid the due on sale clause
- How to "cover yourself" from any liability when you buy "subject to"
- Seven techniques to find "subject to" deals
- The two most common seller objections to these deals and how to handle them
- 24 key clauses you need to protect your interests and maximize your profits
- How to cultivate private funding sources for your deals
- How to flip your deals for instant cash
- And much more!

PLUS you'll also get a FREE bonus CD-ROM containing all the essential documents and contracts you need to safely and profitably buy subject to the existing financing.

Here's a partial list of what you'll get on your bonus CD-ROM:

- Agreement to Sell Real Estate (Buying)
- Promissory Note (Buying)
- Grant Deed
- Warranty Deed
- Quitclaim Deed
- Assignment of Contract (Flipping Deal)
- Limited Power Of Attorney
- Land Trust
- Assignment of Beneficial Interest
- Appointment of Successor Trustee
- "Cover Yourself" Disclosure Letter to Seller
- Acknowledgment of Assignment and Release of Liability
- Authorization to Release Information
- Authorization for Direct Payments
- Additionally Insured Agreement
- And much more!

Your Course Comes Complete With:
- Twelve (12) audio CD's
- 315 page manual
- Bonus CD-ROM of all the essential contracts and documents

Catalog Number: 105 How to Find, Close and Sell Properties Using the Existing Financing
Your Investment: $697

To Order See Success Library Order Form On Page 277
Or Call 1-800-952-9585 ext. 825

How to Buy Apartment Buildings With Little or No Money Down!

For creating massive cash flow, there is nothing better than intelligently buying apartment buildings. For example, four years ago, Peter Conti found a 24-unit apartment building that was owned by a motivated seller. He bought that building and others with nothing down using the ideas from this breakthrough new course. That one building alone still puts over $40,000 of cash flow into his bank account every year!

Would you like to have a cash machine like this building? Imagine the freedom and security it will give you and your family.

In this course, you'll learn how to find, analyze, structure, fund, and close moneymaking apartment deals using little or none of your own money.

You'll learn:
* How to find cash generating properties!
* Nine ways to find landlords who are desperate to sell you their buildings!
* Sample marketing materials and scripts for you to use to find money-making deals (includes direct mail pieces, sample ads, special reports, phone scripts!)
* Seven ways to structure your deals with nothing down!
* How to get outside investors to fund your deals for a share of the profits!
* How to increase the value of your new building by 10% in 90 days or less!

- Five biggest ways to lose money with multi-unit deals and how to avoid them!
- How to determine in five minutes or less the value, monthly cash flow, and upside potential of any apartment building
- How to structure a deal so that you'll get the highest possible return on your investment dollar
- Eight ways to lower your down payment
- The best way to use owner carry financing to purchase apartment buildings
- How to develop private sources of low interest funding for your deals
- How to buy apartment buildings subject to the existing financing
- How to manage your apartment buildings to create multiple streams of income
- How to find, train, and oversee a resident manager (including the five biggest mistakes most investors make when using a resident manager and how you can avoid them)
- How to increase the value of your apartment buildings to maximize your profits when you're ready to sell
- Nine easy ways to increase your building's income
- Three secrets to getting more money when you sell
- How to create a lifetime cash flow and pass all your equity to your heirs without any capital gains tax
- How to find apartment buildings at 20-35% below value!
- The hidden opportunities in multi-unit investing
- 22 Reasons apartment building owners must sell fast
- 17 Expenses every property has (and how to tell when the seller isn't being honest with you)
- How to take control of standard Realtor contracts by using addendums (Includes templates and samples)

- Three secrets to avoid signing personally on a note
- How to get "the inside edge" at every closing
- 25 critical clauses you need to know when you are buying or selling a building
- How to handle the four biggest seller objections that can kill your deal
- 28 Power negotiating tactics when buying apartment buildings
- 20 Things you must do when you are selecting a tenant (and 24 things to avoid!)
- How to set up an effective tracking system to make sure you get your rents in on time
- How to improve your property by getting rid of your worst tenants
- 27 Ways to increase the cashflow from your buildings
- Five additional profit centers in your properties that most investors overlook
- 12 Ways to lower "verifiable" expenses (and why this helps you make more money when you sell)
- 26 Ways to save money on repairs and maintenance
- When it makes sense to use a real estate agent to help you sell (and five things to watch out for when you do)
- And much more!

Plus you'll get sample copies of all the paperwork, forms, and contracts you'll need to invest in multi-unit properties including:

- The Apartment Building Investors Due Diligence Checklist
- Property Evaluation Worksheet
- Earnest Money Promissory Note
- Commercial Master Lease Purchase Agreement

- Memorandum of Option
- Offer to Purchase
- Onsite Assistance Agreement (annual and short term)
- Notice of Change in Terms of Tenancy Letter
- Late Fee Notice
- Maintenance Tracking Form
- Maintenance Request Form
- Tenant Upkeep Violation Notice
- "Bad" Tenant Rent Increase Letter (to encourage them to move)
- Letter to Get Non-Paying Tenants to Move
- Friendly Eviction Letter
- Notice to Terminate Tenancy Form
- Mutual Agreement to Terminate Tenancy
- Form to Use With Eviction Service
- Property Inspection Form
- Move Out Worksheet
- Lease Agreement

FREE BONUS: CD-ROM with the Instant Income Evaluator—a simple yet powerful analytical tool that will help you spot great deals and have the confidence to grab them.

This stand alone PC-based software program will help you do a lightning fast analysis that will show you the cash flow, estimated expenses, actual value, and upside potential of any building!

Your Course Comes Complete With:

- 10 audio CD's
- 382-page manual with contracts, forms, letters, and sample documents
- PLUS Bonus software program

Order now and you'll also get this bonus audio CD course: ($297 value)

"Nations Top Experts Reveal 651 Insider Secrets on Landlording & Tenant Law"

Includes 5 audio CD's:
- Tenant/Landlord Law - Part One
- Tenant/Landlord Law - Part Two
- Mr. Landlord on Investing
- Real World Property Management - Part One
- Real World Property Management - Part Two

Catalog Number: 106
Your investment: $2,497

To Order See Success Library Order Form On Page 277
Or Call 1-800-952-9585 ext. 825

The Intensive Training Video Library

For the past seven years, we've hand picked a few hundred investors and trained them on our most powerful investing techniques and strategies. These investors paid between $4,000 to $6,000 to attend this intensive 3-day training workshop.

Now for the first time ever, you'll get to see exactly what these students learned and save thousands of dollars too! It's like having a front row seat to this 3-day investing workshop all from the comfort of your own home.

There's no expensive travel or hard-to-get time off work. When you're ready to learn these money-making ideas you just put in the tape, press "play" and sit back. Nothing could be easier.

You'll learn how to create multiple streams of income buying homes in nice areas with nothing down!

All totaled, you get the following 15 videos—three full days of investing strategies and "how to's"—as part of your new video library:

Tape One:
- Reasons Why Purchase Option Investing Will Make You Rich!

Tape Two:
- How to Tap Into Hidden Markets of Motivated Sellers—Again and Again!

Tape Three:
- How to Get Sellers to Call You...Begging to You to Buy Their Property!

Tape Four: • How to Find the Deals No One Else Knows About!

Tape Five: • 21 Ways to Make Your Investing Business More Profitable!

Tape Six: • How to Structure Your Purchase Option Deals for Maximum Profits!

Tape Seven: • How to Close a Nothing Down Deal in 90 Minutes or Less!

Tape Eight: • Wealth Without Risk: How to Write Up Your Lease Option Paperwork for Maximum Safety and Control!

Tape Nine: • How to Know Exactly What to Offer a Seller so That You Both Win!

Tape Ten: • How to Sell Your Property on a "Rent to Own" Basis in Three Weeks or Less!

Tape Eleven: • How to Price Your Properties for a *Fast* Sale!

Tape Twelve: • Five Fun, Easy Ways to Make Up to an Extra $100,000 This Year Investing in Real Estate!

Tape Thirteen:• How to Blow Through Your Investing Fears and Get Yourself to Take Instant Action!

Tape Fourteen:• Street Smart Real Estate Realities: How to Stay Safe Investing in A Rough World!

Tape Fifteen: • The 90 Day Plan of Action: How to Close Your First or Next Deal In 90 Days or Less!

Catalog Number: 200
Your investment: $2,497

Advanced Purchase Option Training
Leveraged Business Systems to Take Your Investing to the Next Level

Have you read all about buying subject to, equity splits, and owner financing? Well this graduate level home study course is your chance to learn exactly how to find, negotiate, and write up all the paperwork for these powerful money making strategies.

Get All the SYSTEMS You Need to Take Your Investing to the Next Level

Successful investors have learned to implement winning systems into their investing business so they get great results--time after time. In this advanced home study course, you learn the exact systems you need to do things like:

- Leverage your marketing efforts to find deals no one else knows about
- Create checklists for all your closings and paperwork
- Leverage your time by setting up the business systems to keep your investing business producing twice the results on half the time and effort
- And much more!

This Course is for Advanced Investors...

Let's get clear. This high level course is not for people who have just gotten started and have never even met with a seller. It's not for a dabbler who isn't serious about getting out there and investing. It is, however, for those who are committed to making real estate pay off BIG TIME for themselves.

To get the most out of this powerful home study system, you need to have a basic real estate investment foundation so you can easily incorporate the high level investing strategies you'll be learning into your own business processes to get the leveraged results you are looking for.

With This Comprehensive Home Study Course, You'll Learn How to:

- Buy subject to the existing financing (and avoid the 11 pitfalls of subject to deals)
- Negotiate and write up equity splits, big money cash closes, and owner carry deals
- Use and write up graduated rents/prices and reverse credits when negotiating deals
- Create a selling machine to sell, rent, or rent to own your properties FAST!
- Make an extra $25,000 selling on land contracts and wrap around mortgages
- Use land trusts and corporations to protect your growing net worth
- Structure your business so you have more free time, make more profits, and maintain a balanced life
- Create a real estate dream team committed to helping your business succeed
- Automate your lead sources to produce multiple streams of weekly deals
- Leverage your investing time so you get full time results in 30 hours or less per week
- Protect the money you make from costly lawsuits, governmental agencies (including the IRS), and creditors
- Make fast cash flipping, joint venturing, and buying foreclosures

- Plus! As a bonus, we'll spotlight 3 successful investors and how they run their business and generate 6 figure incomes investing in real estate and how you can too!

Here's an outline of the course:

Section One: Big Picture of How to Take Your Investing to the Next Level (including spotlight on three investors who earn over $100,000 per year investing 30 hours or less each week)

Section Two: Seven (7) Strategies You Can Use to Buy With Little or Nothing Down

Section Three: 12 Leveraged Ways to Find Motivated Sellers

Section Four: Five (5) Simple Systems You Can Use to Find Great Deals

Section Five: Advanced Lease Option Strategies--Hybrid Equity Splits, Graduated Rents, Reverse Credits, and More

Section Six: Mock Presentation to Real Estate Office to Get Deals

Section Seven: Mock Presentation to Mortgage Brokers and Bankers to Get Deals

Section Eight: How to Buy Subject to the Existing Financing

Section Nine: How to Do All Your Subject to Paperwork

Section Ten: The Subject to Deal Game -- How to Do the Deal from Start to Finish

Section Eleven: How to Flip Deals for Fast Cash

Section Twelve: How to Intelligently Tap Into Owner Carry Financing

Section Thirteen: Mock Real Estate Closing (Learn exactly how to do your own closing on creative deals)

Section Fourteen: Mock Presentation to Wholesale a House (Learn 3 little-known ways to turn your deals for fast cash)

Section Fifteen: The Owner Carry Game - How to "Do" an Owner Carry Deal From A-Z

Section Sixteen: 33 Ways to Create A Buying Frenzy When Marketing Your Properties

Section Seventeen: How to Sell on a Wrap Around Mortgage (AITD) or Land Contract

Section Eighteen: Leverage Business Systems for the Real Estate Entrepreneur

Your Advanced Purchase Option Training Course Includes:

- 540 Page Manual
- 12 Hi Fi DVD's
- 26 Audio CD's
- Bonus CD ROM with the essential contracts/documents
- Bonus DVD of Investor Spotlights
- Bonus CD of Investor Spotlights

Catalog Number 107
Your investment: $2,497

To Order See Success Library Order Form On Page 277 Or Call 1-800-952-9585 ext. 825

Negotiate and Grow Rich!

The single most important skill you need to make money investing in real estate is NEGOTIATION.

With this intensive program, you'll learn directly from Peter and David who are revolutionizing the way investors negotiate things that aren't available anywhere else.

You'll learn how to handle and exactly what to say in every major negotiating situation that you'll ever face as a real estate investor. Plus you'll also learn two powerful models of human behavior that when you apply them will instantly supercharge your results in any negotiation exponentially!

Section One: The Big Picture of Powerful Negotiation
• Why negotiation is such an important skill
• Personal skills assessment

Section Two: The Instant Offer System
• The five steps to get motivated sellers to say "yes" to your creative offer
• The five keys to closing the deal
• Three sure-fire tricks to get the best price
• Seven negotiating pitfalls - and how to avoid them

Section Three: 27 Fundamental Negotiating Skills
• How to build rapport to gain trust and get the deal
• Reluctant buyer language patterns and how to use them
• The secrets of getting or making concessions

Section Four: 32 Advanced Negotiating Skills
- How to use hypnotic language to get what you want
- Six reasons why selective hearing pays off
- How to use personality styles to mold your negotiations

Section Five: Advanced IOS Secrets for Terms Deals
- What to offer on the big four Purchase Option deals
- Seven places to get cash to buy properties
- How to negotiate cash deals for 50 to 75 cents on the dollar

Section Six: Successfully Negotiating Through Realtors
- The 5 pitfalls of using realtors and how to avoid them
- Six things to never tell an agent if you want to close the deal
- Top 12 things you should never agree to when buying

Section Seven: Negotiating at the Closing Table
- How to protect yourself from last minute concessions
- Six ways to control the closing

Section Eight: Negotiating with Lenders, Mortgage Brokers & Other Investors
- How to get the best rate and terms from your lender
- How to beat the bankers at their own game and out negotiate the professionals
- 10 Things you must know when negotiating with another investor

Section Nine: Discounting Debt
- How to get lenders to say yes to your short sale offers
- How to get lien holders to accept pennies on the dollar

Section Ten: Negotiating With Tenants
- Five keys to successfully get your tenant to do what you want
- The single most important law when negotiating with tenants
- How to get property management companies to manage your portfolio for HALF their normal fee for up to two years (this one idea is so simple yet effective it will pay for the course)

Section Eleven: Negotiating With Contractors
- Eight danger signs to watch out for when negotiating a contractor contract!
- How to get the best VALUE for your money!
- How to get contractors to give you fair and honest deals!

Section Twelve: Closing Thoughts
- Using tag team negotiation to fine tune your technique
- Tips for negotiating over the phone
- How to effectively go through your contracts

Your Course Comes Complete With:
- 26 audio CD's and 14 Hi-Fi DVD's - over 18 hours of live training and role playing
- 315 page comprehensive training manual
- BONUS CD-ROM - Transcription of the entire 3-day workshop

Catalog Number 108
Your Investment: $2,497

Buy Foreclosures Without Cash or Credit!

Over the past decade, foreclosure rates have literally doubled in just about every section of the country. Now is the time to learn how to tap into this lucrative niche of real estate. Over this past five years these techniques have literally made Peter and David as well as their students millions of dollars in profits. Now it's your turn!

Here's just some of what you'll learn:

Section One: How You Can Earn up to An Extra $100,000 This Year Investing In Foreclosures
- The real story about why foreclosure rates are going to continue to climb!
- How ordinary people have made tens of thousands from specializing in this niche!
- The truth behind the 3 biggest lies you've been told about investing in foreclosures!

Section Two: The Big Picture Of Investing in Foreclosures
- The specifics on what foreclosure is and how the process works!
- Judicial vs Non-Judicial Foreclosures!
- Which stage of foreclosure is it best to buy in and why?

Section Three: 12 Ways to Structure Your Deals So You Don't Need a Ton of Cash or Good Credit
- How to buy subject to the existing financing whether you plan to hold, rehab, or resell the house!
- Seven sources of funding (five of which won't even check your credit!)

Section Four: Short Sales - How to Make Big Money On Houses With Little or No Equity

- How to negotiate short sales with lenders so they'll take pennies on the dollar!
- Step by step how to create your "Short sale packet" so lenders agree to your offer!
- How to fund your short sale purchases using other people's money!

Section Five: 44 Ways to Find Foreclosure Deals

- How to DOUBLE the response from your advertising without spending a dime!
- How to find desperate sellers for free!
- Six hidden ways to find out about foreclosures BEFORE others!

Section Six: How to Close the Deal With Seller's In Foreclosure

- How to negotiate with seller's who are in default (including exact scripts of what to say to them)!
- How to handle the three most common objections when negotiating with seller's in default!
- How to get the seller to just deed you the house and walk away!

Section Seven: Avoid the 25 Pitfalls the Can Cost You Big!

- The five warning signs to watch out for when dealing with a foreclosure!
- What to do if the seller is declaring bankruptcy!
- 12 Steps to take in your due diligence so you don't get burned!

Section Eight: Seven Ways to Turn Your Deal for a Quick Cash Profit
- How to successfully flip your foreclosure deals!
- Three sources of ready buyers!
- How to use the Internet to turn your properties into fast cash!

Section Nine: Three Strategies to Hold Your New Property for Long Term Wealth Build-up
- Three reasons why you'll never let the owner rent to property back from you!
- How to create hands-off cash flows and big back end paydays!
- How to protect yourself when building your portfolio!

Section Ten: Putting it All Into Action
- Seven-step action plan to get your first pay day in 90 days or less!
- Three things you must invest in to be wealthy!
- 17 Questions you must learn the answers to in the first 30 days of your investing or you're asking for trouble!

If you've always wanted to tap into this lucrative market niche but were afraid because you didn't know all the legalities, this is your chance! With this comprehensive home study course, you'll not only learn how to find and close foreclosure deals, but also how to protect yourself so you make the most profit possible with the least amount of risk.

Coming soon! Pre-order your copy today!

Catalog Number 109
Your Investment: $2,497

Order Form

90-Day Money-Back Guarantee!
If you're not totally satisfied with any learning resource, simply return it for a complete and prompt refund!

At Mentor Financial Group, LLC, we believe so strongly in the value of the educational courses we have created that we stand behind them, guaranteeing your total and complete satisfaction. We know that when you study the materials and apply the ideas, they will help you make more money in all your real estate investing.

All of Peter and David's home study courses are covered by a 90-day satisfaction guarantee. If you are not satisfied for any reason, simply return the materials in re-saleable condition within 90 days of purchase and you'll receive a prompt, courteous refund of your investment in the materials (less s&h).

What is re-saleable condition?

This means that all the materials are in like-new condition with no pages torn or written on, the tapes are rewound, and the forms CD seal is unbroken. Basically, the course needs to appear looked through, but not "used," so that we can provide it to someone else who has invested in the course and will use it to make money.

What else do I need to do?

1) Make sure we receive the course within 90 days of the date you purchased it.

2) Make sure the course is in re-saleable condition (see above).

3) Fill out the return authorization form completely, http://www.resultsnow.com/p2247.html and fax it to the number provided

4) Include the original sales invoice with the materials

It's that simple!
If you have additional questions, please go to
ww.onlineclientsupport.com

Thanks for trying out some of our materials.

Do You Want to Create Multiple Streams of Income Buying Homes in Nice Areas with Nothing Down?

Here is Your 100% <u>Guaranteed</u> Way to Learn How in the <u>Shortest</u> Possible Time!

Friday, 10:23 a.m.

Dear Friend,

You've wanted to get up to speed with real estate investing for a long time now. Perhaps you've either done a few "nothing down" deals yourself or you know other people who have.

Or maybe you've been looking for a way to make money investing in real estate, consistently, but you just didn't know where to start. The very fact that you've read this far lets me know that you're serious about succeeding with real estate.

Right Here in this Letter, You'll Discover a <u>Sure-Fire</u> way to Learn How to Use Real Estate to Create Passive Streams of Residual Income!

And you won't need thousands of dollars or perfect credit either! You can start where you are and with what you have and in 90 days or less you will be on the road to wealth.

You'll learn to put together deals just like some of my past students have.

People like:

Craig and Susan, who did nine deals within their first year working with me. (On just one of their deals they have over $37,500 of locked-in profits!) Or...

Heather, a member of the military, who negotiated her first deal two weeks after starting the program. (This deal alone has over $29,000 of locked-in profit!) Or...

Steve, who got started in the program after his last business went under. He called me after he left a recent closing with a check for over $19,000 in his hand (this was from his third deal in four months working approximately 25 hours a week.) Or...

Reddy, a Chinese American ex-accountant, who recently took me on a tour of some of the beautiful homes she had bought and sold using the Purchase Option system. (She makes well over a hundred thousand dollars a year doing what she loves... real estate!) Or...

You might even hit a home run like I did, **making over $249,000 in just three months** on a 24-unit apartment building that I picked up.

Are you looking for more income, or perhaps just more free time?

The best selling author Harry Dent, predicts in his latest book, *The Roaring 2000's*, that the aging baby boomers are now creating the biggest economic boom ever. And the money to be made in real estate will be made by those who get going now.

In any market in any area, 3 to 5 percent of home owners are what I call "motivated sellers." For one reason or another they need or want a quick solution to a pressing real estate problem.

These homeowners are going to make a deal with someone. It could be with you. And once you learn how to find them and talk with them, you'll be able to help them and make a lot of money doing it.

And you are going to do it without turning into a landlord.

Yep, that's right, you won't have to deal with the day-to-day hassles of tenants and toilets.

This is because you'll learn exactly how to set things up where other people are responsible for all the maintenance. EVERY SINGLE PENNY OF IT!

And it's not just the cost of the maintenance that drives most "landlords" nuts. It's the time factor.

For example, let's say it's a Friday night, you're heading out the door for a nice dinner with that special someone and... BZZZ! Your pager goes off and ruins your nice evening.

That doesn't have to happen to you!

Real estate will take on a whole new meaning because...

**You will learn how to create
passive, residual income!**

You probably won't even own a pager! You'll be able to take time off when you want to. You'll be the one in control of your days. Imagine what that would feel like.

The *freedom* and *security* this gives you and your family is incredible to experience.

Of course, this is easier to say once you've done a few deals. In fact, it's getting those first few deals that stops most folks cold. But remember…

If I Can Do It, So Can You!

I started out as an auto mechanic because I thought that was all I could do. Coming from a family with seven kids, I was the one who was expected to struggle financially.

For many years, I lived up to this expectation, living far below my potential. Yet even during those tough times, I craved more.

All the time I was working for $5.50 an hour as a mechanic, I paid attention to what successful people were doing. Again and again I saw people who had made their money in real estate. And these were average people who had started out like me.

Well, sometimes you need to hit rock bottom before you are ready to make a change. It happened to me one day while I was working in an auto shop. It was a cold Colorado winter and the owner had the heat turned off to save money. It was so cold that my fingers were numb. I looked over at the shop foreman who had just come out of the office with a big, steaming cup of coffee. It looked so good I grabbed a coffee mug out of my toolbox, went into the office and poured myself a cup. I wrapped my fingers around it to try to warm them up.

Just as I was walking back to work the owner came out of his office, looked at me and said, *"Peter, that coffee is for customers only!"*

I felt about two inches tall. Have you ever had someone make you feel like that?

As bad as it felt, that was a great moment for me. I decided right then and there to never be dependent on someone else ever again for my livelihood. Never again would anyone have that kind of power over my financial life.

I thank God things got that bad because if they hadn't, I might never have committed to changing my life. Just like you, I had always known real estate was a great way to create both wealth and freedom. So I finally took the leap and began investing.

It was a struggle in the beginning, but within three and a half years, I was a self-made millionaire.

I guess my real point here is that if I could start out as an auto mechanic who struggled to graduate from high school yet went on to become one of the nations wealthiest people in such a short amount of time, then you can too!

And I want to help you do it. That's why my partner

David and I created...

"The Mentorship Program"

Because I tend to be a perfectionist, we invested the past seven years refining, redesigning, and testing this program so that you could get guaranteed results.

What we found was that the students who followed through with the Mentorship Program consistently put together at least one money-making deal within 90 days of getting started, and many more deals thereafter.

I've worked with people all over the country, like you, who were committed to changing the quality of their financial life forever.

People like **Victoria Hobart**, an out of work secretary, put the Mentorship Program to work to create the freedom and security she had always wanted. **She had more profits in her first deal than an entire year's wages!**

Victoria wrote to me and said:

"When I first got started with the Mentorship Program I was living on unemployment and looking for something new to do. I didn't want to go back to work for someone else again so I decided to give your system a chance... My very first deal looks like it's going to make me about $35,000. Thank you so very much for teaching me how to make big money in real estate!"

Or...

Cindy Leavitt, who called me several months back to ask me if it was possible to have too many deals going at once. It seemed that **Cindy had found six deals in one month's time!** (How would you like to have a problem like that!)

Cindy wrote to me and said:

"I'm not very old, but I'm old enough to know to let people go before me and make the mistakes that I can learn from without experiencing the pain. I have already made enough money to repay the investment I made and within the next two weeks will by tying up a deal that will make me $27,000 profit... I was one of those people who dragged my feet about investing the money because I have a "high maintenance" family of seven and run a family-owned store. I felt that I could not tie that money up right then. I finally realized I needed to take action if I wanted to begin to see profits. The only regret I have is that I didn't start sooner."

This system has worked for so many other investors I know it will work for you.

I don't mean to sugar coat any of this, it takes work.

If you're looking for the newest "get rich quick" thing then you're looking in the wrong place. This system will teach you how to put the power of real estate to work helping you make money and creating freedom. And it's going to take work, patience, and persistence.

Are you willing to put in an average of 10-15 hours a week to talk with property owners and look at houses? Are your dreams worth it? Is your family?

It doesn't matter how good or bad your investing skills are now. The Mentorship Program is guaranteed to transform you into the best real estate investor you can possibly be... and much, much better than you could ever be through the use of any other method.

These techniques are incredibly powerful and profitable. They work for beginning and seasoned investors alike. **In fact, one of the major benefits of these techniques is that you can use them for the rest of your life to *consistently* build your monthly cash flow and grow your net worth.**

After completing your training program, the results you'll see as a real estate investor will allow you to begin living life as you've always wanted to.

You will have learned how to create passive, residual income!

You'll be working where you want, when you want. And you can make as much money as you choose to make. You will be the one in *control* of your financial future.

I'd like you to take a minute and think of how your life will be markedly better when you reach the point of having multiple streams of passive income flowing in. What is one thing you'll be doing differently once you're financially independent?

Are you clear on just how your life is going to change?

Great, because once you understand the secret of creating lasting change, you'll realize that the answer is closer than you thought.

The Secret of Success

The secret is to set things up so there is no chance of quitting when you are almost there. Because for you, "almost" just isn't good enough.

You see, there's something strange about life in that sometimes to reach your goal, you have to endure a few momentary setbacks along the way. I believe that sometimes God just wants to see if you really want it badly enough.

And life is full of people who will go after their dreams **until... until** they get tired; **until** they get bored; or until they just plain give up. **When you really want to succeed badly enough, failure isn't an option.**

And if failure isn't an option for you, and the only "until" in your vocabulary is "UNTIL I SUCCEED" then I want to help you get what you want. (Don't worry, I'll be sharing with you exactly what's in it for me later on in this letter.)

Essentially, we'll be working together much like a master craftsman might work with a beginning apprentice or a world-class coach might work with an Olympic athlete.

The Mentorship Program has
Three Essential Stages.

Stage One: The Learning Stage

Stage one is where you build a foundation of investment techniques and strategies to use in your investing.

You'll spend 2-6 weeks working through a comprehensive home study course (It's called the Protégé Program and you get it for free if I choose to work with you.) You'll use the powerful strategies and techniques you're learning during Stage One to be incredibly successful in Stages Two and Three.

The home study course is multi-media. It comes with five thick manuals containing all the specific how-to details and copyrighted agreements you'll need in your investing. Your course also includes a huge audio library with over 36 hours of workshops that you'll be listening to over and over to lock in all the valuable ideas you'll be learning.

During Stage One, you'll be meeting with your coach several times a week on a conference call. You'll talk through what you are learning so you can customize the system to fit your market and your needs.

The conference calls with your coach will make sure that not only are you digesting all of the powerful ideas at a comfortable pace, but that your coach is right there by your side to answer any questions that might come up as you're going through the system.

This leads to...

Stage Two: The Action Stage

Stage Two is where you learn by doing. You put the ideas into action. This stage even includes a live, three-day intensive training where we'll show you exactly how to put the system to work making you money.

This isn't just a "classroom" seminar, it's a hands-on experience where you will actually BE investing. You'll be making calls to sellers and meeting with property owners.

You see, the whole idea is to get you to do the most important, and often times most intimidating, parts of investing right there at the training.

But rather than make the calls on your own or meet with sellers by yourself, the coaches and other students will be right there with you providing a safety net and making learning easier and faster for you.

This process allows us to observe your progress and to give you immediate feedback and personalized attention. In fact, the closer you follow my advice, the faster you will advance in the direction of your dreams.

And remember, the faster you get up to speed, the sooner you can be making money with your real estate investing. Which is why together we'll move through to...

Stage Three: The Launch Stage

The best way to get going quickly is to get out there and actually make it happen. Stage Three is where we all roll up our sleeves and put together winning deals.

You'll be part of regular Q&A sessions where you'll have support on your deals just by picking up the phone!

When you're out there and you find a lead, you'll simply enter the information from a "Gold Form" (a one page property information sheet) into a password-protected web site that is just for Mentorship students.

You can then connect with one of the coaches to talk through the property with you. We'll brainstorm possible scenarios, role-play what to say to the seller, and help you be laser-clear on your specific next steps with that deal.

Our job is to help take the complicated process of investing and break it down into bite-sized chunks. At every step along the way, you'll know exactly what you need to do next to keep the deal moving along to its successful close. Do you see the power in that?

We'll be taking it one step at a time all the way to the bank!

And because we'll be working so closely together, we can help make sure you stay on track with the proven 90-day plan of action.

Within 90 Days of Leaving the Training, You'll Have Your First Deal Done!

It's that simple. <u>And it's guaranteed</u>. (I'll go into depth about this later.) Here's just a few of the recent results we've seen:

The Johnston's, a married couple, took action putting the system to work for themselves. They got started because they wanted to put their two sons through college. In the past year they have done over six deals. On just one of those deals they **have over $42,000 in locked-in profits!** And they did it working part-time out of their home. They made over $100,000 their first year in the program.

John, a 23-year old construction worker, found his first deal two months after working the system part-time. His profits in his first deal are over **$22,000**. He's gone on to do a total of eight deals in his first year working the system part-time.

<u>And *you* can be just as successful as these people!</u>
Even *more* so.

The Mentorship Program Lasts a Full Year!

We'll coach, guide, and mentor you for an entire year to help you learn to invest the right way from the beginning.

You'll be working hand-in-hand with your own real estate coach who will help you structure and close your deals.

You'll also have access to a "members only" web site that will allow you to stay connected with David, myself and the rest of the team. We'll be there to make sure you're clear on what you need to do every step of the way.

You Get Guaranteed Results!

I'm willing to put myself on the line so that you know you'll get guaranteed results. I'm certain that by following my system, you'll get at least one money-making deal with <u>**at least $10,000**</u> in locked-in profits. Period.

In fact, I am so sure of this that I'll put the *entire* burden of proof on my shoulders by offering you this <u>ironclad</u> guarantee:

Within 90 days of leaving the intensive training portion of the Mentorship Program, you will have completed at least one deal with $10,000.00 OR MORE of locked-in profits or you will get a complete refund of all your tuition for the program!

<u>All I ask from you in order to qualify for this guarantee is that you put in a good faith effort working the system.</u> You simply need to follow the 90 Day Plan of Action once you leave the Intensive Training, and **in 90 days or less, you'll have at least $10,000 of locked-in profits from your investing OR IT'S FREE!**

The action plan calls for you to consistently spend 10-15 hours a week on your investing. When you do this you'll get your deal. You can't help but get your deal. By following the behaviors of winning investors you'll win too!

I want to be clear *why* **I am giving you such a powerful guarantee.** I'm not interested in working with anyone who isn't going after their investing with a burning drive to change their life. If you can't commit to making this happen, putting in the effort, and being open to feedback and coaching as you go, then this program isn't for you.

It's only by you taking action and actively going after your dreams over the long haul, that you'll succeed.

But because you are going after your goals, I am willing

to put myself on the line. I know you can do this. I'm staking my time, energy, and expertise on it. All you have to do is put in your share of the consistent effort.

Either you work the system and get your deal within 90 days of the Intensive Training, or you'll get trained, mentored, and coached for all that time by a self-made millionaire... FOR FREE!

<u>Either way you win!</u> But only if you take action and start right away.

"What's this going to cost me?"

Of course, I charge tuition up-front to work with you. I won't work with anyone who doesn't have a financial commitment to working with me. Would you work with someone who doesn't have a personal stake in the relationship? Where they could just quit and you'd have lost all the time and effort you invested in working with them?

There is a range of three levels of tuition. I don't have time to explain them in detail (and to be frank, I don't know which level would be appropriate for you.) When you call into the office and talk with Jamie (more on this in a moment), the two of you will decide which level is best for you.

And if you're willing to split your first two deals with me 50-50, then the best part is that the tuition is incredibly reasonable, because I'm willing to wait to make a large chunk of my profit for helping you out of the profits on deals we do together.
But we need to put first things first...

The real question is, are you serious about becoming a successful real estate investor? If you're the person I am going to choose to work with then you've probably been thinking about investing in real estate for a long, long time.

If you're the person I'm looking for, your intuition has probably been telling you that this is the chance you've been looking for, you just *know* your time is *now*.

If you've been held back by a nagging doubt that you couldn't do it all on your own, or if in the past you just didn't know how to get started, then it's vitally important that you act now.

If you don't call my office right now, you might very well never get around to it. And think for a moment what putting your dreams on hold forever will cost you.

What opportunities will you miss out on…forever?
What experiences will you be cheating your family out of?
How will this affect you when you retire?

Please don't let that happen to you. Remember what Cindy said earlier. *"My only regret is that I didn't start sooner."*

Don't let that be your regret too. **Pick up the phone and call my office at 1-877-642-3466 and ask to speak with Jamie.** The two of you will spend some time talking things through, asking each other questions, and determining if it really is a fit for us to be working together. It's that simple.

Don't miss out on this opportunity. You'll kick yourself if you do.

The Mentorship Program was designed to help you not only learn what you need to learn so that you can earn what you've always dreamed of earning, but also to give you the specific game-plan you need to make this happen.

You already know that real estate is the *safest* and *fastest* way to make money. Let me take you by the hand and mentor you every step of the way.

<u>Please call only if you are truly committed to creating *wealth* and *security* for yourself and your family right *now.*</u>

You don't have to go it alone out there. Together, we will make certain that you succeed and reach your dreams.

My very best to you,

Peter

P.S. This is your chance to have what you've always dreamed of by investing in real estate with me as your personal mentor. Call my office today and ask to speak with Jamie to see if you're one of the select few people I will choose to work with as part of this unique Mentorship Program. **Call 1-877-642-3466 right now!**

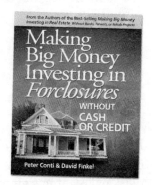

Mentor Financial Group, LLC
7475 West 5th Ave, Suite 100
Lakewood CO 80226

Mentor Financial Group, LLC
7475 West 5th Ave, Suite 100
Lakewood CO 80226

Place
Stamp
Here